DISCOVERING YOUR PASSION

The Path to Your Authentic Life

SHADAN KAPRI

DISCOVERING YOUR PASSION

DISCOVERING YOUR PASSION
Copyright © 2024 by KAPRI PUBLISHING

All rights reserved. No part of this book may be reproduced or transmitted in any form or by any means without written permission from the author and/or publisher.

Kapri Publishing supports copyright laws. Copyright laws encourage creativity, innovation, and diverse voices while protecting ideas and concepts that enrich societies. This is the first edition of this non-fiction book. All rights are reserved except as permitted under the U.S. Copyright Act of 1976.

Printed in the U.S.A

*Names and stories have been changed to protect the privacy of individuals.

DEDICATION

This book is dedicated to my Mother and Father and all the wonderful parents who sacrificed their lives so their children would experience a better one.

A lifetime of gratitude is not enough.

This book is also dedicated to anyone who has ever felt lost while searching for their purpose and passion in life. I remember those days vividly. You are not alone.

May reading this book help you realize there is an important reason for your life. May it provide guidance on your personal journey to find *your* special place in the world.

Don't give up. This world needs you. Now more than ever.

And to anyone who has ever felt limited by society and its superficial labels and roles, may this book help you realize that you are more than just a role or title. You are an amazing spirit who deserves to know its worth. Today. Tomorrow. Every Day.

May you accept this before a lifetime has passed.

DISCOVERING YOUR PASSION

TABLE OF CONTENTS

INTRODUCTION	15
CHAPTER ONE	19
CHAPTER TWO	29
CHAPTER THREE	35
CHAPTER FOUR	41
CHAPTER FIVE	47
CHAPTER SIX	93
CHAPTER SEVEN	103
CHAPTER EIGHT	109
CHAPTER NINE	115
CHAPTER TEN	55
CHAPTER ELEVEN	59
CHAPTER TWELVE	63
CHAPTER THIRTEEN	69
CHAPTER FOURTEEN	75
CHAPTER FIFTEEN	79
CHAPTER SIXTEEN	87
CHAPTER SEVENTEEN	119
CHAPTER EIGHTEEN	127
CHAPTER NINETEEN	133
CHAPTER TWENTY	139
CHAPTER TWENTY-ONE	145
CHAPTER TWENTY-TWO	155
CHAPTER TWENTY-THREE	159
CHAPTER TWENTY-FOUR	165
CHAPTER TWENTY-FIVE	173
CHAPTER TWENTY-SIX	177

DISCOVERING YOUR PASSION

CHAPTER TWENTY-SEVEN	181
CHAPTER TWENTY-EIGHT	186
CHAPTER TWENTY-NINE	193
CHAPTER THIRTY	197

DISCOVERING YOUR PASSION

Other books written by this author:

"The Red Movement: Social and Environmental Justice in the 21st Century"

To learn more please visit www.red-movement.com

PREFACE

As a little girl growing up between two cultures, it always surprised me how much of our lives are predetermined before we are even born. The cultures, families, and times we are born into determine and shape our lives in many ways before our first steps into the world.

Yet, at some point we realize that our life is truly ours. And no culture, role, family, or societal expectation can override that. For many, it happens later in life after many hard-won lessons and steep learning curves. Your life belongs to you and only you. It doesn't belong to your family, your children, or your spouse. You don't owe anyone an explanation for what you love or enjoy doing.

Which brings me directly to why I wrote this book. This is the book I needed to read in my 20s and 30s. My greatest hope is this book will help you find your passion, what sparks joy inside of you. The work that makes you come alive. That is what this world needs. This world doesn't need more successful people. It needs healers, storytellers, peacemakers, writers, and builders of all kind.

DISCOVERING YOUR PASSION

We spend our lives trying to fit in not realizing that our differences are a superpower. People often spend their lives thinking that failure is to be avoided at all costs. Yet, how will you ever find what you are truly capable of if you avoid failure at all costs? Please don't die with your talents trapped inside of you. That's worse than failure.

It's never too late to do your life's work. The activities that you were sent here to do. As long as you have a heartbeat, there is still time. That is why this book was written. That is my greatest hope. This book will bring people closer to why they are here and the activities that make them come alive.

If people can hate for no reason, then I can love for no reason. Wherever you are in the world, no matter what corner, I send you massive love, support, and encouragement. As wonderful as it is to be blessed, *it's even better to be a blessing.*

I've realized in my own life that I often feel drained not because I've done too much, but because I've done too little of what sparks a light inside of me. The activities that make me come alive. Don't Give Up. It's all a process, and one day *your* story will become someone's survival guide, if it hasn't already.

If you are looking for a sign that everything will be okay, then this is your sign. Let us begin. There are dreams out there that need to be given life.

DISCOVERING YOUR PASSION

30 Life Rules
That No One Tells You

Your past does not define you. It prepares you.

Rejection is God's redirection. Better is coming. Be patient.

Trusting someone is the highest compliment you can give to them, not verifying that same trust is the biggest mistake.

The greatest risk in life is not doing what you truly want in hope that you will have the time later. The time may never come unless you create space for it.

There is no such thing as failure. You either win or you learn. Both are victories in their own time.

If you find your way out of life's darkness, return and bring the light to help others.

You become a success when you help others become successful.

Dreams don't have an expiration date, nor a timeline.

Mistakes can lead to blessings and wisdom you never knew existed.

You are not ahead or behind in life. Life is not a car chase or a competition. It's a journey and each journey **is** meant to be different. Seven billion people can't all follow the same timeline nor were they ever meant to.

If you are positive in a very negative situation, then you have won.

Judgements are mere opinions, not facts. Treat them accordingly.

30 Life Rules
That No One Tells You

It's not over when you lose. It's over when you quit.

The only people you need to impress is the five-year-old version of you and the eighty-year-old version of you.

The world is not competing nor conspiring against you. It is merely a reflection of your own thoughts and beliefs.

We are all sent here to help one another. That is our main mission in life. Our jobs just give us an avenue and opportunity to do that.

If you think your life is over, that's when it gets interesting.

Social media is not real. The more people try to show how great their lives are on social media, the more problems they actually have.

Fake friends encourage fake lives. One true friend is better than 100 fake acquaintances.

Loneliness is a universal experience. It can happen to anyone even though we are wired for connection. However, if you feel that you are being excluded by your so called "friends," then let them. They are doing you a huge favor. Only go where you are truly valued. That is the only way to find your true tribe.

The greatest gift you can offer (to yourself and others) is an authentic life. People need the real you. Not a version of you.

Life can be so difficult and challenging that unless you turn your pain into purpose and passion, your tears into triumphs, and your defeats into discipline, this life can embitter you, and then you won't

30 Life Rules
That No One Tells You

be used as a force for good. You could potentially become a force for darkness. That is how your life is ruined.

There are two places that you need to go to often. The place that heals you and the place that inspires you.

No one is you and that is your superpower. Never forget that your differences are your strengths not your weakness.

If you feel like you are losing or in a dark place, remember trees lose their leaves every year and come back more beautiful and stronger the next year. You are no different.

If your pain helps someone else, then it was not in vain. Our real purpose is to help each other along this journey called Life.

There is a past version of you that is so proud of how far you have come.

Every day you are living inside one of your answered prayers. Remember that when things get tough.

What if creating the art and doing the work is the reward? It's not about recognition. It's about doing meaningful work that aligns with your soul and makes you want to get up in the morning. This work has to be created so you can continue to live with purpose and passion in life. If doing the work excites you, then it's worth doing. It's about being true to yourself.
The one person you owe it to...

INTRODUCTION

"Creating—that is the great salvation from suffering." This famous quote by the German philosopher Friedrich Nietzsche (pronounced Nee-Chee) summarizes why finding and pursing your passions in life are essential to the human experience. Discovering your dreams and passions make life worth living even on the darkest of days. Yet, the first step to discovering your passion is to discover what is not meant for you, and this can be heartbreaking.

As you go on this journey, I challenge you to look back on your life and reexamine the times when you thought you were being rejected only to later discover that the experiences were meant to be part of your path so you would learn valuable lessons.

The truth is when we don't get what we want, we are heartbroken. We become confused, frustrated, and angry. We wonder, "Why is this happening to me? Why did life bring me so close to what I wanted just to take it away?"

The part of the story no one talks about is how many years later, we begin to see the divine timing in our lives. We begin to realize how rejection is redirection. Not getting what we want can and does lead to a better life. With time, clarity is recaptured.

Yet, this book isn't about rejection – it's about discovering your passions. However, to get on that path rejection is essential. It keeps people from going down the wrong roads. From loving the wrong person. From picking the wrong careers. From acting in ways that betray their own sense of self.

Millions of people experience this every day but no one talks about it. What if rejection is the Universe's way of taking you down a different path? A better path? A path that is greater than you can ever imagine.

Often when we think we are being rejected we are actually being redirected towards our life's work. The work that can save ourselves and help others. The real reason we are sent here.

Statues

When we gaze upon statues we are trained to think

Those individuals possessed something extraordinary.

Only a few of us will cure any disease or fight mythical dragons.

Yet, in the quiet tapestry of our everyday existence

We are each called to be a leader, a hero, or a helper.

Statues do not just honor the exceptional.

They remind us of what is possible in our own lives.

Mirrors of extraordinary characteristics

That reside in each of us that

Go unused or unnoticed.

DISCOVERING YOUR PASSION

CHAPTER ONE

Discover Your Dreams

"Death is not the greatest loss in life.
The greatest loss is what dies inside of us while we live."
~Norman Cousins

When people fail to pursue or even discover their passions in life, there is a sense of loss they experience throughout a lifetime. For many, it's difficult to put into words, yet, their actions speak loudly. They spend their lives searching for something - a new relationship, a new job, a new city, new friends, a better body, a new marriage, more toys, a bigger house, a better career. They continuously search for that elusive thing that will make them happy. Not surprisingly, they fail to find it in all those things.

In their quietest moments, when no one is around, they release frustration and anger at themselves and the world that robbed them of the life they always wanted. Some even drown their sorrows down a bottle or at the end of a pill container.

How often does this happen?

Every. Single. Day.

In all likelihood you and I know someone like this. Yet in our soul, we *know* this is the path taken when one abandons their own dreams and aspirations *for the sake of others*. Discovering and pursuing one's passion does not solve all of life's problems. It just helps make life worth living.

The first step in discovering your passion is to rediscover and acknowledge those dreams deserted long ago. The reasons may differ: responsibilities, money, family obligations, life problems, marriage. The stories may be different but the ending is the same. To discover your passion, you need to go back. It's ironic how we watch other people live out our dreams, yet we lack the inner faith to live them out for ourselves.

Some may even say, "What if I don't know what my passion is anymore? What if I've lost sight of it after taking care of my job, my kids, my partner?"

I'll let you in on a secret. You are not alone.

Everyone (including myself) has felt this way at some point in their lives. For me it was in my 20s. I spent most of my 20s feeling lost. Trying out different careers and different cities just to find they weren't a good fit. Every change broke my heart because I thought it was *the life or the career* for me. This happened because I was listening to everyone *but myself.*

DISCOVERING YOUR PASSION

The easiest way to mess up your life is to listen to everyone around you while ignoring the small voice inside of you that has been there all along, patiently trying to guide you. Some call it intuition while others call it a sixth sense. Regardless of the terminology, it's the voice that comes to you unexpectedly when you really need it, but you ignore it because there is no direct proof or evidence to support it.

Many spend their lives ignoring that voice. Sometimes it even goes away after decades of casting it off. Yet, now is the time to bring it back.

Before we get ahead of ourselves, let me introduce myself. My name is Shadan Kapri (pronounced Shadawn Capri). I am currently an attorney and writer. (Please no attorney jokes.) I've dedicated my life to human rights issues and human trafficking awareness.

Yet, I spent most of my 20s feeling lost while searching for my place in the world. I felt like everyone else had a place except for me. I watched my friends' graduate college, start careers, get married, and have kids while I was still trying to figure out what to do with the rest of my life (and often the rest of the day).

Did I feel lost? Yes.

Did I have a Quarter Life Crisis? Yes.

Was it frustrating? Absolutely.

Did I retreat into my own world as a way to heal what I thought was intrinsically broken about me? Yes. Did it help? Not really.

It wasn't until my 30s that I finally realized that my journey was independent of anyone else's. It was independent of the family I was born into, the culture I grew up in, and the opinions and judgements of everyone trying to give me good advice.

DISCOVERING YOUR PASSION

It was in my 30s that I realized something life changing. There is a special place for you and me in this vast world that no one else can claim. Why? Because no one else is you. No one else has your unique set of experiences, skills, and background.

You are not summoned to your unique path, you are invited down a rabbit hole that is independent of what your parents say, or what any teacher has told you, or even what your friends and family may think.

This path is yours and yours alone.

It belongs to no one else.

There will be times when you are tempted to settle for less and take the easy way out. Please don't fall into that trap.

Your path belongs to you and only you. If you try to be someone else, another version of someone who already exists, then you will fail over and over again because the world already has them. The world needs you, and the experiences and skills that only you bring to the table. Your unique place in this world doesn't belong to anyone else. No one can be you.

The purpose of this book is to help you find that place.

There is nothing more demoralizing than someone who gives up on themselves. Someone who gives up on their dreams and allows the passions inside of them to slowly die or worse yet never really begin because of other people's opinions and judgements.

Your path may not make sense to anyone else and *it's not suppose to*. It was never a conference call. It was never meant for them to understand. The fastest way to kill any dream is to tell everyone about it. This has killed more dreams than failure ever could.

Some days you may feel like you are crawling forward. Other days you may run. Regardless, move forward every single day even if it's just an idea or a single action. One day you will look back and see how far you've come and you'll be astonished at your own progress.

As Mother Teresa so eloquently stated, "Yesterday is gone. Tomorrow has not yet come. We have only today. Let us begin." I'm with you every step of the way. Let's begin to find your place in the world.

You need this but more importantly *the world needs you*.

No one is you and that is your superpower.

To help with this process, there will be a **Soul's Journal Entry** at the end of every chapter. These are opportunities to ask yourself questions that have likely never been asked before. There's space available to answer those questions in the book, and in the e-book version there is a place you can type the answers (in notes).

You can read through the book and answer the questions at the end of each chapter, or you can wait until the very end to answer them. I believe the best way to use this book is to take one chapter at a time. This provides ample opportunity to ponder and answer the questions at the end of each chapter. If you want to read the book in one sitting, that is encouraged as well.

Regardless of the technique, the answers to those questions can reveal your passions and give you insights into what you truly want, who you can become, and the path that will lead you to your authentic life.

DISCOVERING YOUR PASSION

Your answers are the most important part of this book. Finding your truth is the key to all of this. It takes courage to answer the questions honestly. There are no right or wrong answers. Only right or wrong answers for *you*. When it comes to affairs of the heart, only you know your truth.

There is a place in your heart that has been waiting for this for a long time. There is a better life waiting for you. Let us begin.

Soul's Journal Entry #1

Find a quiet place to gather your thoughts and begin to answer these questions. If the answers do not come to you, then move onto the next question and come back to answer them later.

May you find what you are searching for.

Ultimately these are answers only *you* can provide.

During my childhood I really enjoyed the following activities:
_____
_____
_____

During my teen years these activities brought me joy:
_____
_____
_____

This is what brings me joy as an adult:

DISCOVERING YOUR PASSION

_____
_____
_____

I always wanted to _____
_____

but was afraid I was not good enough to _____
_____

I have always fantasized about
_____
_____
_____

My one desire that I have never shared with anyone is
_____
_____
_____

Before I die, I would like to do this (it can be anything):
_____
_____
_____
_____
_____

DISCOVERING YOUR PASSION

These are the dreams I would like to pursue if time was not a factor _____

_____
_____
_____

I can overcome obstacles to achieving these by _____

_____
_____
_____

If my life had no limitations, this is what I would do in a heartbeat.

_____
_____
_____

This is my truth that I've never shared with anyone. (If you can't answer this then come back later.)

_____
_____
_____

Dreams

Fear kills more dreams than failure.

It ruins more lives than drugs or alcohol.

Only you know what is right for you.

Your calling or passion is not meant for anyone else.

It was never meant to be a discussion.

If was only meant to be understood by you.

Otherwise, it would be *their* dream or passion in life.

DISCOVERING YOUR PASSION

CHAPTER TWO

Rediscovering Yourself

*"Nature never repeats herself,
and the possibilities of one human soul
will never be found in another."
~Elizabeth Cay Stanton*

Finding your passion is more than just unveiling your truth, it can also be a rediscovery of who you were before society's labels and expectations took hold. Unfortunately, all too often in life, we begin to believe the labels and roles that are bestowed onto us by others. We become the Mother, the Father, the Wife, the Husband, the Provider, the Son, or the Daughter. Yet, there's so much more to us than those limiting labels. Do those labels even come close to describing who we really are inside? The answer is "no." They never will.

To find your passion, you need to rediscover who you are. Not within the roles that others see you. Not within the roles society defines for you, but who you are as a spirit on a spiritual journey. Who you are as a soul that cannot be boxed into limiting labels and other people's expectations. A soul that ultimately wants to experience freedom. Freedom doesn't come from working in a cubicle or checking off a checklist that society has arbitrarily created.

By finding and pursuing your passion, you give your soul a chance to finally express itself in the form *it sees fit*, and not in the expectation or the roles created centuries ago. That is why finding your passion through a rediscovery of yourself is an important step. It forces you to stop looking through other people's perceptions and finally search for your truth. That is what your soul has wanted all along to realize that other people's perceptions do not define you.

This message became clear one cloudy afternoon. While having coffee with an old friend, her words surprised me. "How can I rediscover who I am when I feel I have disappeared? All that is left is mother and wife. Any trace of anything else has been lost," she pronounced adamantly.

In all my years of knowing her, I had never heard her say such words. Yet, I realized that she had never expressed these feelings because no one had ever bothered to ask. People had asked about her children, her parents, her new home, her job. Yet, no one bothered to ask about her. *Who was she outside of the context of mother, wife, daughter, confidante? Who did she want to become? What were her dreams independent of everyone else?*

In all the years I had known her, it shocked me to my core that I had never once bothered to ask. I felt ashamed. Yet, I wasn't going to let my shame let go of this opportunity. The opportunity for her to speak to me for the first time without reservation or judgement.

We would end up talking for hours about who she was, who she wanted to be, and what she hoped to become. I realized that an important step in discovering your passion is to realize the roles have eclipsed you. Instead of being part of the role – the role becomes you. We weren't born to live roles dutifully. We were born to live.

Soul's Journal Entry #2

Find a place that is quiet and you feel comfortable. Then begin to ask yourself these questions.

What are the ways that other people see me?

_____
_____
_____

How is that different from who I really am inside or how I see myself?

_____
_____
_____

What are the parts of myself that have been suppressed by the roles defined by society?

_____

DISCOVERING YOUR PASSION

_____
_____

What can I do to bring my true personality to the surface?

_____
_____
_____

Who do I see myself as being separate from these roles?

_____
_____
_____

If this question is hard to answer try to remember back at who you were before these events or roles?

Why do I allow other people's perception of me to have such a huge impact on the ways I view myself?

_____
_____
_____

How can I avoid that in the future?

_____
_____
_____

What is the one thing I want everyone to know about me that I keep to myself?

DISCOVERING YOUR PASSION

_____
_____
_____

My Hope for You

May your path be as smooth as the sands of time.
May your journey through this life be gentle and kind.
May your heart be strengthened and your soul satisfied.
May you find love every day of your life.

May you realize the answers have been deep inside of you.
May you accept those answers have always been true.
May you face your darkest nights with the courage of a fighter.
And finally realize you truly are a survivor.

May you discover your dreams and your heart's desire.
May you pursue them with an everlasting and eternal fire.
May you live your life with the awe of a child,
Not with regrets for all your tribulations and trials.

May you deeply experience this journey called living
For the saddest conclusion is not in its ending.
It's coming to the realization
There was never really a beginning.

CHAPTER THREE

Listen to What is Happening Inside of You

*"The soul has no secret
that the behavior does not reveal."
~Lao Tzu*

One of the sad ironies of life is that we spend so much time focusing and listening to the ones around us that we often know them better than we know ourselves. In the noise of the external world, we become experts in deciphering others, reading their emotions, anticipating their needs while neglecting the hollow chambers of our own heart.

DISCOVERING YOUR PASSION

We live in a world that does not encourage us to listen to what is happening inside of ourselves. Instead, it encourages us to fill every waking moment with distractions. Distractions as to why we are truly here. These include everything from watching television, movies, gaming, shopping, and even obsessively scrolling the internet at night. I am absolutely guilty of all of these.

In fact, if given the time, some people would have no idea what to do with themselves if they were not working or engaging in some form of distraction. In other words, they would go crazy if they had to sit in silence, and try to listen to what is happening inside of them.

"Wouldn't it be boring," I often hear.

The answer is "no."

Not if you listen close enough.

To find your passion, you must begin listening to what is going on inside of *you*. It is then that you realize your passion has been inside of you this whole time, yet it's been quieted through the years by the countless distractions, responsibilities, judgements, and opinions of others.

Instead of burying those feelings with distractions or even drugs and alcohol (the most destructive of all the distractions) you can face them and begin to understand the real reasons for your behavior and your intentions. You can begin to heal.

If you ignore something long enough, it will go away. Yet, if you create space for it in your life, it will come back. This is the beauty in listening to yourself. You come back smarter and stronger than you ever were before.

DISCOVERING YOUR PASSION

Soul's Journal Entry #3

Find a place that brings you comfort and sit in silence. Light a candle if you have one. Then begin by asking yourself these questions. Wait for an answer. If you do not receive one, ask another question until you begin receiving answers. They will come in time.

When I sit in silence I feel? _____
_____
_____

What do you really want?
_____
_____
_____

What does that look like for you? _____
_____
_____

What can you do today to become one step closer to that?
_____
_____
_____

Ask yourself what you have been doing wrong and how you can rectify those mistakes. _____
_____
_____

DISCOVERING YOUR PASSION

Ask yourself to guide you and how will you know when it is doing so. If you feel resistance, ask yourself why _____
_____
_____
_____

Ask your soul the deepest question that you have always wanted to know the answer to _____
_____
_____
_____

What kind of societal conditioning do you need to un-learn?
_____
_____
_____
_____

How will you feel afterwards? _____
_____
_____
_____

What is stopping you? _____
_____
_____
_____

DISCOVERING YOUR PASSION

Comes the Dawn

After a while you learn the subtle difference
Between holding a hand and chaining a soul.

And you learn that love doesn't mean leaning
And company doesn't mean security.
And you begin to understand that kisses aren't contracts
And presents aren't promises.

And you begin to accept your defeats
With your head held high and your eyes open,
With the grace of an adult, not the grief of a child.

You learn to build your roads
On today because tomorrow's ground
Is too uncertain for plans,
And futures have a way of falling down in midflight.

After a while you learn that even sunshine
Burns if you get too much.
So you plant your own garden
And decorate your own soul,
Instead of waiting for someone to bring you flowers.

And you learn that you can really endure,
That you really are strong
And you really do have worth

And you learn and learn.
With every goodbye you learn.

~Jorge Luis Borges

CHAPTER FOUR

Listening to Life

*"Don't be afraid that your life will end.
Be afraid that it will never begin."
~Grace Hansen*

One of the greatest puzzles in life surrounds a simple truth. Many people fail to really listen to their lives until they are about to die. It is then that many experience a sense of clarity that was missing throughout their life. An understanding of what was there all along. Yet, the process of dying should not be the catalyst that makes an individual listen to their own life.

The truth is that your life has been communicating with you the whole time. It communicates with you in small ways, in large ways, and in ways you don't understand until years later. It communicates with you through the people that you meet, the experiences you have, the pain and suffering along the way. It talks to you in moments. When you listen to your life, you begin to see the reverence and wisdom in everyday occurrences. You begin to understand the realities of your own soul, and in the process, you begin to unveil *your* truth.

One of those realities surrounds the people who find their way into your life. It is no coincidence they share their journey with you. They are meant to cross your path. Each and every one of them has an important life lesson to teach you. Yet, how often do we really learn?

The next step in discovering your passion or soul's desire is to listen to your life. It serves as a tool to guide you through your darkest moments and offers wisdom in your happiest ones. It provides clarity into who you really are and what your passion truly is.

It can also grant an inner-peace by understanding that the Universe strives to teach us and not just cause pain and suffering. It is in our darkest moments that we gain our greatest insight into who we are, why we are here, and the journey that can finally lead us home. Not home in a physical sense or a structure, but a place where we are comfortable within our own skin and don't need the outside world to feel validated. A place some never find because they are too busy chasing other people's dreams. A place that has brought you here.

The importance of this life lesson became evident the day I met Michelle. Michelle was a charming and insightful 75-year-old woman who initially taught me the importance of listening to my own life. She spent a lifetime ignoring the signs. "At first they were very subtle," she would tell me, "In hindsight, they were there all along."

Michelle shared that throughout her life there were many lessons that she needed to learn. Mistakes that she should have avoided all because of her unwillingness to listen and learn from her *own* life. All because of her inability to see experiences and people for what they truly were - meaningful opportunities to learn. She saw "red flags" as cute quirks. She interpreted subtle and not so subtle jealously as acts of love. She didn't see her own worth until much later in life.

In her wise and benevolent way, Michelle taught me the importance of listening to my own life. I realize that each chapter in life can feel like many lifetimes. The importance exists in learning from each of them.

For as the seasons change, the pages of our life slowly begin to turn. These pages are integral and significant as the book itself. They hold the key to our passions in life.

To find your passion you need to begin by listening to your life. The people in it, the experiences, and the pain as well. By listening to your life, you become closer to who you really are. It does not lie in possessions, money, status, or power. It lies in something much more real and precious.

It lies in you.

Soul's Journal Entry #4

Make a list of the people in your life and the lessons they have taught you. Have they taught you the importance of knowing your worth, patience, honesty, self-reliance, or have they taught you what not to

DISCOVERING YOUR PASSION

become? Make this list as long and detailed as possible to understand their contribution to your life. This list can be ongoing.

Below is an example of an outline that may be helpful.

NameExperienceLesson Learned

_____ had a profound impact on my life, he/she taught me the importance of _____ through the experience of _____

They brought me closer to who I really am by teaching me that

_____
_____
_____

This experience taught me to _____
_____
_____

How can this knowledge help you find your passion?

He or she made me realize that _____
_____

What will you change in the future?
Different things I will not do in the future because of this experience:

DISCOVERING YOUR PASSION

DISCOVERING YOUR PASSION

CHAPTER FIVE

Recognize Your Destructive Voice

*"Learning too soon our limitations,
we never learn our powers."*
~Mignon McLaughlin

    We all have it. That voice inside of us that tells us that we are not good enough, smart enough, pretty enough. We can't do it. It's too hard. We may fail. I called it the destructive voice, for that's exactly what it does. It destroys dreams, aspirations, and desires before they are even given a fighting chance. It robs people of the struggle to even try. A struggle that can be just as a rewarding as the attainment of the goal itself. In short, it robs people of their passions in life.

An important step to recognizing your passion is to learn how to silence that voice. It causes more pain, disappointment, and frustration than anything else. This was driven home to me the day I met Susan. Her sadness screamed from her eyes. Her despair could be heard in her voice.

Susan was a 32-year-old single mother with two children and two jobs. Her passion life was to become an artist. Since her childhood, she kept this passion a secret from almost everyone who met her because her father had criticized her talents.

Yet she opened up to me. She began by talking about her difficult childhood. An alcoholic father and a passive mother who had survived on the outside, yet spiritually died years ago.

She expressed how the mental abuse at the hands of her father still stung after two decades, yet the physical abuse had healed many years ago.

It did not take long for me to realize the intelligence and insight that Susan possessed, yet I knew it would take a lifetime for her to accept this herself.

Throughout her life, she had constantly been told that she was not good enough, smart enough, or talented like her older sister. Sadly, she began to believe it. Her father had really wanted a boy. In her mind, she had been cursed from the very beginning.

As I listened to this intelligent, emotionally wounded soul, I began to realize how the destructive voices we hear decades ago can often still ring in our ears today. My heart bled for the little girl who had heard those messages and for the woman who still believed them today.

Now more than ever, I believe that to find your passion in life, you must learn how to silence that voice inside of you. All it really fosters is a sense of fear, inadequacy, and despair. It holds no real purpose or value.

Those messages are not from a divine source.

In a way, it keeps people in their own prison. A prison of perpetual self-doubt, fear, and insecurity. A prison where some remain their entire lives.

Throughout the afternoon, Susan and I discussed how she could still become an artist today. She could create art every day, yet that didn't mean she had to quit her job or drastically rearrange her life.

Your passion doesn't have to be your whole life. It doesn't have to be your career. It can be what you do to find peace and solace after a long day at work. It can be what you do during the weekend or weeknights instead of scrolling the internet or watching T.V.

People often think that finding their passion means quitting the job that pays their bills. This is furthest from the truth. We need different parts of our lives to provide us with different needs. Your day job is just as important as your passion. If anything, it may help balance your life and bring you that peace that can't be found in any other way. We all need our day jobs and our passions in life. One does not eclipse the other. Each has its own place in our world. They can work together to give us the balance so desperately needed today.

Soul's Journal Entry #5

How can you pursue your passions while also keeping your day job?
_____
_____
_____

What is stopping you from doing that?
_____
_____
_____

What were the destructive voices you heard as a child?
_____
_____
_____

What kind of impact have those had on your adulthood?
_____
_____
_____

What are the destructive voices you tell yourself today?
_____
_____
_____

How has this impacted your life now?
_____

DISCOVERING YOUR PASSION

_____
_____

How has this helped you?

_____
_____
_____

If it hasn't helped, then why have you listened to them?

_____
_____
_____

How has it impacted the way you view yourself?

_____
_____
_____

How has it impacted your relationships?

_____
_____
_____

How has it impacted your soul?

_____
_____
_____

DISCOVERING YOUR PASSION

What can you do to eradicate it (the destructive voices)?
_____
_____
_____

What will your life be like after they are gone?
_____
_____
_____

What is stopping you and why?
_____
_____
_____

What can you do today to finally know your worth?
_____
_____
_____

The Stage

We often look at other people's lives and
Believe they have what we want.
Their life is somehow better, more fulfilled,
Maybe even charmed.

Yet, do we really know them?
Do we know the realities behind their closed doors?
When there is no one else to lie to.
No one else to fool.

For some people, their entire life is a performance,
On Facebook, Instagram, even TikTok
For their friends, family, and even themselves.

A performance that often begins to fade as they get older,
When they realize the time they've wasted away.
So the next time you look at someone else,
Don't envy them for the real story
May be lost on the stage.

DISCOVERING YOUR PASSION

CHAPTER SIX

Search for Your Truth

*"You will never find yourself
until you face the truth."*
~Pearl Bailey

Look for the truth in your life. Not the truth the media tells you or your friends tell you, but your truth and you will begin to find your passion. It astonishes me the number of lies, half-truths, and false hopes we tell ourselves. The excuses we make for others when we wouldn't grant ourselves the same grace for the same offenses.

"When people show you who they are believe them the first time." When I first heard this quote from Oprah Winfrey during a college graduation speech, I stopped for a moment. It had a profound impact on me. I realized that so many people flee from the truth in themselves and others because it holds harsh realities they would rather leave hidden.

To find your passion, you need to look at those half-truths and realize how lying to yourself and others impacts you. When we don't look at the truth, then our lives became a mirage of half reality and half deception. After some time, the two can become merged into a sea of denial. Then our lives become hidden behind a mask of false illusions and lies.

To uncover your soul's desire, you must look at those illusions and uncover the truth along with the reasons you have been running away from them.

This life lesson became even more evident when I met Jenny. At the age of fifty-five she was finally facing the truth about her life, and she did not like what she saw. Unlike what the outside world had imagined, she felt stuck in a high stress job and marriage that was on the best days bearable and on the worse days - soul crushing.

One night, between the gulps of wine, she was finally ready to acknowledge how the demands of her life were becoming unbearable. She had never dared to say those words out loud because it felt too raw and real.

She had lost her passion for life and felt exhausted 98% of the time. To make things even more complicated, her intimate relationship with her husband had practically dried up. This created even more tension and problems in their marriage.

As a little girl, she had imagined her marriage would be very different, and for as long as she could remember, she had fooled herself into believing it was.

Years later, Jenny shared how she found the truth in her life. She began writing in a private journal every day that no one knew about. She would spend a couple of minutes writing down whatever came to her mind throughout different parts in the day. She then wouldn't read the entries until the end of the week. And every week she began to see common themes that would arise.

It was from those writings that she began to find the truth. She began to peel back the expectations of others and realize how she really felt and thought. And she uncovered all the anger and resentment she was carrying around inside of her and how it was poisoning various aspects of her life and her self-esteem.

It was from those journals that Jenny rediscovered her love for writing and began to create nonfiction stories as a "release" from the demands of life. Searching for the truth taught her about herself along with her actual needs and desires.

What could searching for the truth teach you?

<u>Soul's Journal Entry #6</u>

Spend several minutes at different times throughout the day writing down whatever comes into your thoughts (DO NOT censor it and DO NOT show anyone).

Let this be an opportunity for your soul to express itself freely without limitations or considerations of other people's feelings or judgments. These writings are private so please keep them in a secure place. This will give your spirit the power to be completely honest and forthright.

At the end of the week, look back at your writings and search for common themes or topics that you keep visiting. Think about how these issues have been affecting your life and health. They can uncover amazing insights into your soul and what it actually needs.

Create a safe space for yourself where you can vent and give yourself praise for all the things you are doing well in life.

Keep this journal in a secure place. It is only meant for you as a way to release your emotions in a safe space that doesn't hurt anyone or create more friction in your life.

CHAPTER SEVEN

What Excites You

*"We come into this world
with a song in our hearts that we need to sing
before we die. That is our passion."*
~Carol Carr

If you had to look back on your life, did you spend most of it doing what was expected of you or what really excited your spirit? For most of us, the answer will be the former.

On our final day, will it really matter? Will it really matter that we spend the better half of our lives doing what was expected? Will it really matter that doing what excited us, what made us feel alive was on the bottom of our list? Will it really matter that we spent our lives running in circles waiting for the day when we could finally do what we wanted? You better believe it will.

On our final day, our last day on this earth, no one will thank us for our selflessness. No one will remember the sacrifices we made along the way, and the difficult journey we lived through. No one will remember but us.

Therefore, to each and every person reading this, I ask you, no I beg you to do something that excites your soul every day. It can be something as small as taking a bubble bath, or something larger like enrolling in the art class that you have been thinking about. Do not let another day go by that you pass the opportunity to do one thing that excites you. You will never get that day back. It's a wasted opportunity that stops today.

A wise man once said, "When tomorrow comes, this day will be gone forever, leaving in its place something that I have traded for it. I want it to be gain, and not loss; good, and not evil…in order that I shall not regret the price I have paid for it." By finding and pursing your passion, you will never regret the price that was paid.

A good way to rediscover what excites you is to begin with a list. A list of all the activities you enjoyed as a child, adolescent, and now an adult. For some individuals, this may take a considerable amount of time for they have buried these activities under many years of expectations and high ideals of what they "should" be doing.

To help you get started here are a list of some activities.

Which ones jump out at you?

    swimming, yoga, meditation, writing, cooking, painting,

    sculpting, stain glass, pottery, singing, poetry, bubble baths gardening, interior design, acting, entertaining, teaching, planning parties or special occasions, photography, scrapbooking, crafting, shopping, hiking, rafting, horseback riding, taking care of animals, time by the water, jet skiing, traveling, sewing, sleeping, watching documentaries or movies, exercising, running, mountain climbing, white water rafting, downhill skiing, snowboarding, cross country, hiking, camping, working on cars, working on motorcycles

Soul's Journal Entry #7

Make a list of all the activities you enjoy doing. _____
_____
_____
_____

Are there common themes or activities that you have enjoyed your entire life? _____
_____
_____
_____

How often do you participate in these activities? _____
_____
_____
_____

Is that often enough? Why or why not? _____

DISCOVERING YOUR PASSION

_____
_____
_____

What is stopping you from enjoying these activities? _____
_____
_____
_____

How can you overcome those obstacles? _____
_____
_____
_____

What will your life be after that? _____
_____
_____
_____

CHAPTER EIGHT

Childhood Passions and Perfect Days

*"The past is never where
you think you left it."
~Katherine Porter*

In many cases, people discover their passion as children, yet for a variety of reasons are discouraged into continuing them as adults. Children do not carry around the anger, resentment, and pain that adults often do. It's much easier for them to find and pursue their passions. They just don't possess the emotional baggage that can stall the process. Yet, as children, we are trained early on to do what is expected as a way to survive in this world. The downside is that this can and does kill a passion.

DISCOVERING YOUR PASSION

As a little boy, Jamie loved painting and drawing. He would take every opportunity to create. Yet, this was continuously discouraged by his parents as he became older. He had more important tasks to focus on and help with around the house. It wasn't until years later that Jamie would rediscover his passion for art. A passion that had been trapped for years.

For some, rediscovering their passion can be as easy as remembering their favorite childhood activities. Activities that brought them happiness, energy, and joy. As we age, these activities are often replaced by the everyday demands of life. Yet, in order to have a fulfilled life, we need to find space in our lives for these activities. In order to have a satisfying life, we need to incorporate them back into our normal routine. This doesn't mean we go out and quit our jobs to become struggling artists. Instead, it means we create time and space in our busy lives to do the things that brought us joy as children.

One of my favorite quotes of all time was in the movie, "Under the Tuscan Sun." In one scene, an older wiser woman is giving the main character life advice. She eloquently states, "Never lose your childlike enthusiasm." This quote stayed with me many years later because of its simplicity. When we lose our enthusiasm for the things that make us happy and curious, then we lose a part of ourselves. And some spend decades trying to excavate those parts back.

Throughout our lives, we live through thousands of days. Yet, how many of us would trade a few of them in for that one perfect day when we feel truly alive?

A helpful exercise that provides greater insight into your passions is to determine your perfect day. How would it start off in the morning? What would you do during the day? Who would you visit or would you spend it alone? Where would you go and with whom? Most importantly, when was the last time you had such a day? One month, one year, ten years? The usual response is, "I have responsibilities – my job, my kids, my life!" That is a true response, but wouldn't they all still be there? Wouldn't they want to see you happy and revitalized?

Of course they would.

This topic may become one of the most important in determining your passion or passions in life. It can show you that you periodically take part in your passion, but that you don't take it very seriously or create enough space for it in your life.

This entry can become the pathway into your soul's desires. The activities you would take part in if time, money, and responsibilities were not a factor. Everyone deserves at least one perfect day in life.

It amazes me how many people do not know their passions yet in detail can share their perfect day. What they would do, where they would go, and with whom they would do it with. This was the case with John. He had no idea what his passions in life were. As far as he was concerned, his life revolved around his job, his children, and his wife. If he had any time left over during the day, he would either read or stare half awake at the television set.

Yet, when I asked about his perfect day, his response was immediate. He enthusiastically outlined the day and all the activities he would participate in. He would begin by sleeping in, then cooking a delicious breakfast, going for a hike in the mountains with his wife and children while taking pictures. He would then have a delicious lunch and begin reading his favorite book. In the afternoon he would go for a swim, create some art, and then have dinner with his best childhood friends.

After he explained his perfect day, I looked at him with a smile and said, "So you are telling me that you don't know what your passions are in life?"

DISCOVERING YOUR PASSION

Passions don't have to be writing or creating music. It involves activities that you love and make you feel alive. It doesn't have to be fancy or expensive. It just has to feed your soul and make life better – no matter how small.

Soul's Journal Entry #8

Make a list of your childhood passions. All the things you loved to do as a child. Make this list as long as you possibly can. If you have problems remembering, ask your relatives (sisters, brothers, parents, cousins) about the activities you loved to do as a child. They will likely remember and possibly spark your memories.

_____
_____
_____
_____

Describe your perfect day:

In the morning, I would
_____
_____
_____

In the afternoon I would
_____
_____
_____

In the evening, I would
_____

DISCOVERING YOUR PASSION

_____
_____
_____

How would you feel at the end of the day?
_____
_____
_____

Believe in Yourself.

Believe in your inner strength
That will carry you through the darkness
And sustain you in the light.

Believe in your value
For you possess an
Irreplaceable and priceless soul.

Believe in your intelligence
For you are a fountain of wisdom,
And a wealth of understanding.

Believe in your power.
For the biggest fear is not the fear of failure.
It is the realization of the untapped potential within you.

Believe in your passion,
It is the pathway to your soul.
Believe in Yourself.

CHAPTER NINE

Your Ideal Self

*"It's never too late to be what
you might have been."
~George Eliot*

I believe that we all have an idea of our higher self. This is the best version of us. We have all met someone like this in our past. This person has overcome his/her obstacles, faced their demons, and come out stronger and wiser because of them.

Yet, very few people ever feel that they have reached their highest self. Instead, they often feel that they journey between the person they really are and the worst version of themselves.

It doesn't have to be this way.

Your ideal self is the person you were destined to become. It is part of the reason you are here. Reaching this challenge may take a lifetime, the reality is that most people never get there. To begin with, they have no real notion of who their ideal self is. Instead, they become the worst version of themselves. Their pain, trauma, and exhaustion is dumped onto the people they love the most. They allow life's challenges to weigh them down instead of build them up. They become the opposite of their ideal self – pessimistic, cynical, sarcastic, angry, bitter, spiteful and even jealous. Then they try to bury it with drugs, alcohol, or any distraction that is self-defeating. We all know someone like this.

Yet, by having a clear notion of your ideal self, you can begin the journey to becoming that person, and in the process your passion will appear.

In my mind, a clear example of this was Sarah. Sarah was a forty something divorcee. It had taken her too many long and difficult years before she had finally broken free from "the marriage from hell."

Even after the divorce, she was not sure who she married. The marriage had left her financially, emotionally, and spiritually barren. It had taken every ounce of courage and strength to finally leave. "I knew that if I didn't leave one of us would die," she told me, "And I was afraid that would be me."

The mental abuse had started very subtly in the beginning yet the physical abuse is what stung the most. "It was a slow progression; it wasn't as if he woke up and slapped me one day. It took years before it led up to that. Yet, the red flags were all there from the beginning."

She recalled the control and guilt that he would use on a daily basis. He always wanted to know where she was, who she was with, and what she was doing. Ironically, she had more freedom living in her parents' home than her own.

Later he began to isolate her from family and friends. She thought this was the price for love. Yet, there was always a price that she had to pay. He didn't lose anything.

When I met Sarah, she was still reeling from her feelings of anger, self-pity, and resentment. "The physical scars healed years ago, but the psychological scars still sting." Yet, the tone in her voice and the look in her eyes told me that she didn't want this to influence the rest of her life. "What is the point of leaving a marriage if I am going to relive the trauma every other day?" she shared.

She had physically left the abusive relationship; she didn't want to remain in it emotionally and continue to bleed. "If I allow what he did to me to affect the rest of my life, then I have never really left. I have just avoided the bruises."

For the next two hours, we would talk about her ideal self. The person she would have been without him, the person she wanted to become. She took a long hard look at herself, and the obstacles standing in her way. She decided that by taking the journey to become the best version of herself, then she could finally become free. "It would be as if he had never been in my life."

Now isn't that the best revenge of all? Living a happy life as if they never existed and hurt you.

Soul Journal's Entry #9

Write a list about your ideal self. Who is this person? What kind of qualities does he/she possesses. Describe them with as much detail as possible.

_____
_____

DISCOVERING YOUR PASSION

_____
_____
_____
_____
_____

Write a story of their typical day. What kind of life do they lead? Where do they live? _____
_____
_____
_____
_____

How do they deal with their problems? _____
_____
_____
_____

Are there times when you have become your ideal self (shown the same characteristics and qualities)? If so, when has this happened?
_____
_____
_____

What can you do today to become one step closer to your ideal self?_____
_____
_____
_____

DISCOVERING YOUR PASSION

Make a list of the things you can do every day to bring you closer to your ideal, authentic self?

_____
_____
_____
_____

What times or events make you feel less than your ideal self and how can you respond differently? _____

_____
_____
_____
_____

DISCOVERING YOUR PASSION

CHAPTER TEN

Listen to Your Intuition

*The future often seems like an
unknown, dark, and slippery path.
Intuition is the light that
leads you through it even
when the road seems bleak.*

One of the most precious gifts we are given is intuition. Too often people ignore, suppress, or doubt this innate ability. They believe that because it cannot be "proven" in the strictest sense, then it's not worth following. Intuition cannot be explained or proven yet neither can love. As a result, do people ignore or suppress those feelings as well?

Of course not.

Your intuition is the most powerful tool you have at your disposal 24/7. It will bring more insight into situations and people than your mind and heart combined. It will keep you from getting hurt, and help you find your true passions in life. Other than your soul, it is the most important gift that you are given while on Earth. There is a reason you have it, therefore, begin to use it. Realistically, if you owned a home, would you never live in it?

The more you begin to listen and honor your intuition, the stronger it will become. When looking back on your life, have you ever regret not listening to your intuition? Have you ever done the opposite and later felt foolish? Millions of people have and will continue to do so unless they begin to listen and trust their intuition. These innate abilities have served us for countless generations, and they will continue to serve us for generation to come.

Intuition often comes out the strongest in our personal relationships. This was the case when Paul met Sammie on a dating app. There were red flags from the beginning. She incessantly talked about her ex-boyfriend while punishing Paul for things her ex had done to her in the past. She had never taken the time to heal and instead jumped from one relationship to another. A pattern she had continued for most of her adult life.

On the outside, she looked like an ideal partner. She was smart, funny, witty, and kind. But behind those crystal blue eyes, were demons that had never been dealt with. Instead of taking the time to heal, she would bleed all over the next person who would come into her life. And then wonder why no relationship lasted.

Paul knew that Sammie had issues that she needed time to resolve, however, he was head over heels in love with her. She made him feel alive and while he was terrified of her, at the same time, he felt exhilarated while around her. She had this magnetic energy that no one could deny, but his family watched from afar with serious concerns. Every time they would bring these concerns to his attention his response was that once they were married her insecurities would melt away.

Yet, the opposite happened after their marriage. Instead of feeling more secure in the relationship, she felt completely raw and vulnerable. She would lash out at him for the slightest mistake. He knew quickly into their marriage that it wasn't going to last. The mental abuse become more common while the physical abuse began to rear its ugly head. He was too embarrassed to let anyone know, but deep down he knew that he had to let her go no matter how much it would hurt.

By ignoring his intuition from the beginning, it caused him more pain in the long run. Many people ignore their intuition because it would force them to make changes in their lives. Changes on what they are doing, who they are with, and the path they are on. Changes that are hard in the short run, yet, ultimately provide more security and satisfaction then staying in a toxic relationship.

Don't worry that your life will change. Worry that it will always stay the same. For that is the true path to never realizing your passion. The activities that make you come alive under the mundane tapestry of everyday life.

DISCOVERING YOUR PASSION

Soul's Journal Entry #10

Looking back on your life, have there been times when you ignored your intuition? What are some examples?
_____
_____
_____

What were the results of ignoring your intuition?
_____
_____
_____

What did you learn from those experiences?
_____
_____
_____

Are you willing to listen to your intuition in the future? What do you think can be gained? _____
_____
_____
_____

CHAPTER ELEVEN

Regrets

*You can often identify a person by their regrets,
some wear them on their face,
others hid them in their hearts,
and some seal them in their souls
next to their addictions and vices.*

For as long as people have existed, regrets have been an integral part of the human experience. For many, they can be as revealing as their fingerprints and last just as long. They often burden the soul with memories of disappointment and frustration. Memories that can and often do last a lifetime.

DISCOVERING YOUR PASSION

An important step in discovering your passion is to recognize your regrets and determine why they are there. The small ones that bother you, and the large ones that keep you up at night. If not recognized and constructively dealt with, regrets can have a profound impact on your life, health, and well-being. They can destroy passion and keep you in a prison of perpetual self-doubt, disappointment, and unhappiness. There's a reason regrets are in the past, it's best to keep them there.

The impact of past regrets became even more apparent when I met Stacie. She was a thirty-four-year-old partner in a national law firm who worked around the clock. She revealed how she lived to work. Everything she did evolved around her job leaving very little time for anything else in her life. She often spoke of her large office, generous bonuses, and company perks, yet by the tone of her voice and the look on her face, it was evident something was missing.

For many months, I waited for the appropriate moment. The time I knew she would be the most honest. The moment her walls would disappear. When the time arrived, I gently asked her, "So what are you running away from?" She did a double take and replied with a smirk, "What makes you think I'm running away from anything? Why would I run?" She glanced around nervously at the room and quickly changed the conversation. The subject turned to a new case along with her aspirations within the firm.

It wasn't until two weeks later that I unexpectedly received a call from a voice I barely recognized. A voice so frail and filled with sorrow that I initially assumed it to be a stranger. My disbelief at her identity startled her. Her story would startle me. She asked if we could talk, and it wasn't until that moment that she began to tell me her story.

During her third year of college, she had met someone. She instantly felt a bond with him as if she had known him her entire life. They shared countless hours together and it flourished into love. "He was everything I wanted to be," she shared. Where she was loud, he was laid back. Where she was conservative, he was spontaneous. Where she was blunt, he was diplomatic. He completely understood her, and she in turn completely adored him. Within a short period of time, she had fallen completely in love and dreamed of a future together. A future that would never be.

He had never really known the extent of her love, and neither had she until he was about to leave. "I'll never forget it. I was sobbing and he had his head tilted away from me. I broke the cardinal rule. I told him that I would do anything, be anyone, if he would just stay," she said with strain in her voice.

They both knew it was over. He had taken a job out of state and she was moving on to graduate school. Their lives had taken completely different paths.

"A part of me regretted not following him. When the relationship ended, I fell apart. I felt I was dying inside. The feeling of loss and devastation was overwhelming." To avoid the pain, she plunged herself into her graduate studies and later her career. Yet, at the end of the day there was always something missing, a part of herself that she couldn't get back no matter how hard she tried.

As the conversation continued, she shared her disgust for the person she had become. She felt weak for her willingness to do anything to keep him. She tried to rectify that by going to the opposite extreme by becoming a strong, independent, career-minded woman. Yet, her regrets were still affecting her life today. She was finally able to face this once she let the façade fade away.

She began to share how her regrets at losing that relationship had impacted her life. She had not been able to maintain a close relationship with any man longer than three months, and she had continuously used her career as an excuse to keep people at a distance. Yet, deep down she wanted someone in her life again.

"You need to let him go," I gently said. "As long as you hold on to this regret you will never really move forward. You may do well professionally. To the external world, you will continue to thrive, yet personally you will continue to be emotionally trapped and stunted. While longing for your past, you will lose out on a different future."

On that fateful day we both learned a very important life lesson. If you let go of your regrets, you can regain your life again. "He will never know how much he hurt you so why do you keep holding onto it? What does it solve?"

"Send him a good-bye letter."

"What?" she replied with a blank look on her face.

"What's a good-bye letter?"

"A good-bye letter is one you wrote for yourself to him but you never mail it. It's a chance to say goodbye to the hold he has on you. It's a chance to break free and start over again. This time for real."

A few weeks later she called me and told me that she cried while writing the letter. It took her three times before she could finally finish it.

"In a strange way, I feel like something has lifted," she said, "A burden I was carrying around has finally been released."

Who do you need to say goodbye to?

Soul's Journal Entry #11

Do you have a good-bye letter you need to write?

Find a place that is quiet and you can be alone. Bring some tissues with you and start writing the letter. It can be very difficult at first and you may hesitate in writing it. Remember no one has to read it. This letter is for your soul to finally end that chapter of your life. No one has to see the letter but you. Afterwards burn the letter or tear it up. The letter is for you and no one else.

Notice how you feel afterwards. Do you feel better? Like a sense of release from something that you didn't even know was weighing you down? You may be surprised.

Another idea is to divide your life into sections. Some people use decades as delineations while some use watershed events like weddings, births, starting a new career, even moving. It can be any life event that holds significance for you.

Then write a list or story of the "regrets" in each season of life. Write several sentences (or more) of how these regrets have impacted your life today.

Have they made you more cautious?
Have they made you less trusting?
Have they left you angry and resentful inside?
Have they created emotional walls that are impermeable ?

DISCOVERING YOUR PASSION

Have they stopped you from living the life you have always wanted? How have these regrets impacted you? Only you know the answer to these questions. No one else can help you.

The last part of this journal entry is to think about how these "regrets" may have turned out for the best. Did they teach you life lessons? Did they make you stronger, more empathetic? Did these regrets help you connect to others going through the same situation? How have these regrets changed you for the better? Have they directly or indirectly revealed the truth about you or someone in your life? Have these regrets made you wiser?

Make a list of the byproducts of these regrets. The unexpected gifts they have given to you. The reason for this part is very important because it teaches us the importance of regrets. Their purpose is not just to cause us pain but provide guidance and insight.

What have your regrets taught you?

How have they made you stronger?

What would you say to your younger self going through those events?

Write these out and keep the journal entries private.

No one else needs to see these. They are yours and yours alone.

DISCOVERING YOUR PASSION

The Path

Looking back on my path of life,
I begin to see things with a sense of clarity.
The road was very windy and
often times I felt lost
only to later realize that this was the path
I was destined to cross.
There were potholes and detours along the way.
I stumbled and fell many times.
Yet each provided valuable lessons and
clues to watch for on my way.
There were people who hurt me
and people who helped.
All as vital as the journey itself.
There were roadblocks that dampened my spirit,
and hardened my soul.
Yet with time I learned to use them not as stumbling blocks
but as stepping stones.
There were moments that I needed to rest
with the full understanding that my path had to continue.
Yet when I get to the end of my voyage
I hope I don't say this with a sigh.
For it to end without realizing my true dreams is
the saddest of all crimes.
This path was created just for me.
My own journey I needed to live.
Yet how many times did I truly understand this?
How many times did I truly live?

DISCOVERING YOUR PASSION

CHAPTER TWELVE

Tribulations and Trials

*"Adversity causes some men to break,
others to break records"*
~William A. Ward

For as long as I could remember, Sara feared adversity. Feared that it would dampen her spirt and break her soul. That it would leave her weak and fragile inside. That it would ultimately break her. For a short period of time, it almost did.

At the young age of twenty-one she was diagnosed with the onset of rheumatoid arthritis. An autoimmune disorder that can have devastating effects on the body's joints and immune system. In some cases, it can leave its victims in wheelchairs or bedridden. She knew this firsthand because that is what it did to her uncle.

It all started in her junior year of college. For several days at a time, she would lose function of her fingers and wrist. She had no idea what was wrong and on some unconscious level she didn't want to know.

Yet, during her junior year of college the unthinkable happened. She lost her ability to walk for four long days. In retrospect, that was the beginning of a new chapter in her life.

Soon afterwards there were a series of doctors' visits and tests, waiting rooms and x-rays, questions and forms to fill out. All to find out what was wrong. All to find out what could be done.

When the news finally arrived, it sent her into a spiral of perpetual denial and anger that lasted well over two years. Two years of her life she can never get back. Two years that she still regrets. Yet, those two years were essential. The old version of her had to die before a new one could be reborn. That was the only way she could survive.

It would take high doses of drugs that made her feel worse, long days in bed, nights filled with tears before she would finally accept the truth. In many ways, she felt broken inside for having this illness. She spent many nights wondering why this had happened to her.

"How will I get my life back?" She would often wonder during her darkest moments. Looking back, it took tiny steps. It wouldn't happen overnight. It wouldn't happen for years, yet in her heart she knew it would happen.

A year later she was accepted into a prestigious graduate program. A lifetime of sacrifices, hard work, and dreams had finally paid off. Yet, how could she do it? How could she handle the demands of the program and this disorder? How would she survive? These were all questions that kept her up at night, but she was too afraid to share them. Afraid to show her internal weakness. Frightened to reveal her deepest thoughts.

After many hours of consideration and prayer, she finally decided that she could not walk away from her dreams, from all those years of hard work. She would not allow this illness to get the best of her.

Several months later, she began the graduate program. A new chapter was about to begin. A different journey was starting to unfold. "Looking back that first year was the hardest, most painful year of my life to that point. I was in a new city far away from my family in a program that completely overwhelmed me." She felt isolated and alone in addition to being sick.

There were many times that she felt broken inside, inadequate, and fragile. Many times, when she just wanted to go home. Yet, she knew the hardest journeys are also the most rewarding ones. They are the ones that bestow the greatest wisdom and strength. They are the ones that build character and resilience. She persevered and suffered silently all in the hope that this path would teach her life lessons.

Many years later she would go back to those days in her mind and realize that in life the greatest tragedies can turn into the greatest lessons. It all depends on how they are dealt with. She has often expressed that becoming sick has been the greatest teacher of all.

"I have learned more from being sick than I could ever learn from being healthy." It bestowed a sense of understanding, empathy, and compassion that made her a better person. Ironically, years later it would help her in her career as well since she could understand

DISCOVERING YOUR PASSION

the difficulties her patients would go through. A young woman who felt broken for having an illness would later feel whole for experiencing it.

That is the mystery and beauty of life. What starts out as a tragedy can later become a connection with others in a profound and meaningful way.

"I have been able to connect with my patients because I understand what they go through. In that sense it was an unexpected gift that would take years to reveal itself."

Soul's Journal Entry #12

What has been your greatest tribulation or trial to date?
_____
_____
_____
_____

How has it changed you?
_____
_____
_____
_____

What has it taught you?
_____
_____
_____
_____

Has it made you closer to who you really are? Why or why not?
_____
_____

DISCOVERING YOUR PASSION

In an ideal world, how do you feel it could have changed you? (What would have been the best-case scenario in terms of its impact on your life?)

Have you used your tribulations and trials as a chance to grow stronger and wiser or more bitter and numb? If no, what has stopped you?

How do you want this journey to change you?

Who do you think you can become?

DISCOVERING YOUR PASSION

CHAPTER THIRTEEN

What Are Your Intentions?

*"Most people are so busy knocking themselves out,
trying to do everything they think they should do,
that they never get around to what they really want to do."*
~Kathleen Winsor

Our passion comes out of our intentions in life. As Gary Zukav explains in *Soul Stories,* are your intentions to be happy, loving, and giving person? If so, do your actions mirror those intentions? If not, they could be killing your ability to find and pursue your passion in life. Some individuals carry around anger, resentment, and disappointment like a scar on their soul. They hold onto it for years because they believe it keeps people at a distance and prevents them from getting hurt again. Yet, it's almost impossible to find your true passion in life, the real reason for your existence, with that excess emotional baggage weighing you down every day. It covers your soul with layers of feelings that are self-destructive and self-defeating.

It's almost like searching for a treasure under a pile of junk. The junk has to be moved in order to find that one perfect treasure. This holds true for your passion as well. If you are living within the walls of anger, disappointment, and resentment, how do you expect your soul's desire to shine through? You have to peel back those layers of pain before you can find your passion. Before you can begin living the life of *your design* (and no one else's).

Passion is expression of the soul at its highest form. I'll repeat that again, passion is the expression of the soul at its highest form. Anger and resentment bury passion within the walls of your soul. By beginning to tear down those walls, your passion has a chance of finding its way to the surface again.

This lesson became even more evident after my encounter with Monica. Monica was a 52-year-old mother of three, who found herself experiencing the "empty nest syndrome." With her husband gone all day at work, and no kids attend to, she desperately wanted to find and pursue her passion in life. Yet she had absolutely no idea what it was. After many attempts at different workshops, classes, and endless hours of discussion, she felt hopeless. She clearly felt that she had used up all her resources and come up completely empty-handed.

When I came into her life, she was finally ready to confront the issues of her past. With a little reassurance, her story began to pour out of her soul.

DISCOVERING YOUR PASSION

Throughout her 34 years of marriage, she had felt very alone. Her saving grace had always been the children, and she had invested every ounce of herself into them. She and her husband had been living parallel lives for as long as she could remember, and the pain had not been as sharp until her children began to move away. It was only then that she began to confront the past. The feelings of loneliness, emptiness, and inadequacy that had plagued her an entire lifetime

On top of it all, she learned that while she was tending to the children, her husband had carried on an affair. This burned her to her core and left her feeling foolish and angry inside. After quietly listening to her story, I realized that her feeling of betrayal, hurt, and disappointment weighed heavily on her every day, and had subsequently buried her passion alive.

She did not have the children to distract her anymore. All she had was the truth. For as long as she could, remember, her life had been about other people. Yet, now, the anger would not allow it to be about herself.

In reality, she was angry at her husband, and herself for the life they had led together. On the outside, it seemed like the perfect union, yet on the inside it was a storm gaining turbulence with each passing day. She felt cheated out of the life she could have had. She felt betrayed for the life she did have. Yet, I knew that she would never uncover her passion and finally be free until she faced her feelings of anger and betrayal. Until she faced the truth.

I tried to begin by explaining that passion was the expression of the soul at its highest form, yet the pain and anger was preventing that passion from ever surfacing. In many ways, her soul was suffocating inside because of it. Until she faced the feelings of anger and resentment, she would never really be free.

I also explained it in terms of a storm. When the storm leaves, the rainbow has the opportunity to shine again. It's when the pain begins to leave the soul that the highest form of expression can come through. That is when your passion will resurface because of the space created for it to survive.

Soul Journal Entry #13

What are your intentions in life?

_____
_____
_____

Are those intentions mirrored in your actions?

_____
_____
_____

What kind of anger, resentment, or pain are you carrying around in your life and why?

_____
_____
_____

How is it affecting your health, life, well-being?

_____
_____

DISCOVERING YOUR PASSION

___

What would it take for you to heal?

___

How can you begin today?

___

Accountability Exercise

The next exercise was created by Lonnie Bradley, and it helps individuals recognize and release the anger, fear, and sadness they carry around with them every day. I personally had the opportunity to see this at work, and was amazed by the results. You can do this by yourself or have someone guide you through this by asking the questions. Both methods work well.

1. Scan your brain to see where you are holding feelings.
   Stomach = Fear
   Neck and Back = Anger
   Chest: Sadness and Regret

2. Take several deep breaths and focus on breathing into the discomfort.

DISCOVERING YOUR PASSION

To yourself say, "This is the way (anger, fear, or sadness) feels." Write down what it feels like.

_____
_____
_____

3. How often do you feel this way?

_____
_____
_____

4. Write down what you are feeling and the emotions it brings to the surface?

_____
_____
_____

5. Tell yourself the story (the details of what happened from your point of view).

_____
_____
_____

6. Ask yourself, "What should or shouldn't have happened in your perspective and why was it unfair to you?"

_____
_____
_____

DISCOVERING YOUR PASSION

7. Explain to yourself the other person's point of view (as if he/she was standing in self-defense explaining what they did).

   _____
   _____
   _____

8. Now ask yourself, "Now what?" Be willing to see the big picture. Take responsibility for your part in the problem as the other person sees it. Ask yourself, "What did I do to help set this up? What was my role in this?"

   _____
   _____
   _____

9. Acknowledge your part and ask yourself, "What am I willing to release and let go of to be happy again?"

   _____
   _____
   _____

10. Ask yourself, "How will I grow from this experience?"

    _____
    _____
    _____

11. Remember the qualities, skills, attitudes that have gotten you through your hardest times before? What can you apply in this situation to help you through this?

12. Visualize (in detail by using your senses) the changes in yourself that you anticipate. See yourself walking through this difficulty and coming out of it a better, wiser person because of it. What does that look like to you?

DISCOVERING YOUR PASSION

The One

Our entire lives, we are taught to search for the "One."
The "One" who is supposed to make our lives complete.
The "One" who will shower us with love.
The "One" only for us.

Yet, often when we find the "One,"
Life gets in the way, bills need to be paid,
Children need attention, others seek our time.

In our quietest moments by ourselves we begin to wonder
If he/she really is the "One?"
Was it all an illusion? Did I make a mistake?

For some the years of heartache and disappointment
Begin to wear on their face and burden their soul.
And only a few in their wisest moments
Begin to realize that the "One"
They had been searching for was with them all along.

It was there through their darkest days.
It was there when their heart was breaking.
It was there when no one else knew
What they were really going through.
The "One" they were looking for
Was with them all along
Staring back at them the whole time.

DISCOVERING YOUR PASSION

CHAPTER FOURTEEN

Live Your Life

*"It is easier to live through someone else
than to become complete yourself."
~Betty Friedan*

One of the best ways to never uncover your passion is by living your life for or through others. When you do this your life becomes about their wants, needs, and desires. Ironically, you become closer to what their passions are than that of yourself.

The saddest of all realizations is coming to the end of your life only to realize that you never lived it for yourself. You never lived their life for them and you never had the chance to live yours either. Everyone realizes that you never get a second chance to live once.

Yet, does everyone truly incorporate that idea into their day-to-day existence? Rarely.

The first step is to realize this mistake. The second step is to find the strength to break free of this pattern. This was the wisdom Beverly taught me on our fifth conversation together. She began by explaining how her life had become a series of other people's desires, wishes, and demands. She would often watch her daughter talk endlessly of college life and the demands of her classes, only to envy the challenge and the opportunities she never had.

After many years, and several "light bulb moments," she realized that she had been living her life through everyone else's but her own. At first, this was a very uncomfortable and even bitter realization for her to accept and finally acknowledge.

Yet, she sacrificed herself for her family. "Wasn't that noble?" She asked me on a cloudy afternoon while sipping on peppermint tea. I looked her firmly in the eyes and gentle responded, "no."

How could she ever expect her children to be independent and happy when she had never done it herself? How could she ever expect to find her passion in life? Is that what she wanted for her children? To sacrifice their lives for the next generation as she had sacrificed her life?

She then looked me in the eyes and firmly said, "no."

Yet, once she got over the initial disappointment and discomfort of this idea, she decided to stop wasting another moment of her life and began pursuing a dream that had always been waiting for her.

At the age of fifty-six, Beverly decided to go back to college and study creative writing. At first it was a very difficult transition. She was older than all of the students in her classes and felt very out of place. She also endlessly worried about all the years she had been

DISCOVERING YOUR PASSION

out of the "system." Yet, with hard work and an undying thirst for knowledge, she graduated four years later with honors. A distinction she still beams with today.

"So how do you feel now?" I would ask her many years later. "I feel that by sacrificing my life for my children and husband, indirectly I was also sacrificing theirs as well. My underlying anger and disappointment would come out in the most unexpected times and places."

She went on to explain that through her actions, she was telling them constantly that she wasn't happy with her life, and for all they tried to do to compensate, it was never enough. It never would have been enough. "How could I ever be happy with them when I was never really happy with my choices in life? I feel that I freed us all."

Soul's Journal Entry #14

Sit in silence in a comfortable location and begin asking yourself these questions.

Have I been living my life for and through others? If yes, in what ways has this happened? _____
_____
_____

What purpose did this serve?
_____
_____
_____

How has this impacted me?

How has it impacted the way I see myself?

How has this impacted my family?

Do I want to continue this? Why or why not?

What can I do today to stop this pattern?

What has been the downside of this behavior and what have I learned?

DISCOVERING YOUR PASSION

If I could go back, what would I tell my younger self?

_____
_____

DISCOVERING YOUR PASSION

CHAPTER FIFTEEN

F-O-R-G-I-V-E

*"Holding on to anger is like grasping a hot coal
with the intention of throwing it at someone else,
while you are the one who gets burned."*
~Buddha

For so many, finding their passion remains inherently difficult because of the feelings of anger, betrayal, and injustice that weigh down on their spirit every day. These layers of destructive emotions keep them from finding their true voice and the ability to find their passion because they are too focused on the pain.

Forgiveness is one of the most difficult things humans can do. It's also one of the most important. Many believe that by holding onto the anger or disappointment, the other person somehow is punished, but this is furthest from the truth. The only person who burns is the one holding onto anger. The source of the anger often doesn't even know how much suffering they have caused.

Forgiveness is the highest form of healing that a soul is capable of. It is the highest form of self-love that your soul can express for its own well-being. When a person forgives, they consciously make a decision to free themselves from the perpetual pain that infested their life. Many times, they fail to realize how this pain impacts almost every facet of their lives from their relationships to their own mental and physical well-being.

In fact, study after study has shown a direct link between our emotional and physical well-being. One cannot be impacted without affecting the other as well. When we forgive, we finally break those chains that keep us in perpetual darkness.

I truly do not believe that people were given this precious life to be angry, mean, or spiteful. Or to hurt others and make them feel inferior or unworthy. These responses are all byproducts of their own pain and suffering that spill onto others.

Instead of learning from their pain, they become it. Instead of walking away a better person, they allow themselves to become engulfed by it and thereby bitter. They key word being "allow."

Often people don't realize that they must forgive others for stealing their peace of mind. Instead, anger is followed by more resentment and the cycle escalates creating chaos, confusion, and even self-harm. They allow this to happen because it takes far more strength and insight to walk away from a disheartening and devastating situation as a smarter and better human being than as an angry, vengeful one.

They allow the pain in their past to control their future, thereby becoming a prisoner to it. The only one who truly suffers is themselves. For they have to live with that pain until the day they die unless they learn the powerful lesson of forgiveness.

Forgiveness doesn't mean the other person is off the hook. It doesn't mean the misdeed didn't happen. *All it means is that you won't allow their actions to imprison you in negativity any longer. For the longer you hold onto anger, the more you punish yourself.*

The power of forgiveness was driven home to me by the story of an amazing woman who forgave the man who had killed her son. While listening to her story, I was astonished at her ability to forgive. I secretly wondered how she was capable of such an act. Someone asked if she harbored any anger or resentment towards the man who had caused a car accident and then abandoned her son to die. No, she shook her head gently. She first explained that this act of forgiveness did not occur overnight. It took a considerable amount of time and reflection. She then began to tell her story.

She shared how her son's death had been the most devastating aspect of her life. She did not want to live after it happened. The mere thought of waking up in the morning made her sob. She could not envision her life without him.

She later introduced us to a mother who also had lost a child. Her daughter had died in a horrible accident as well. Initially, she had blamed everyone who was there for her daughter's death, yet, years later she realized that by blaming others she continuously perpetuated the pain that was deep inside of her. She explained that the anger was inside of her like a fire and by blaming others it continuously fed the flame.

"The pain will never go away, the fire will aways be there, yet the act of forgiveness made it easier to live. When I chose to forgive, I was doing it for myself and my daughter. I knew that she would not want me to live this way because ultimately hating others was destroying my own soul."

She went on to share that for her to have any quality of life possible she needed to forgive, for her own sake. "I know my child would have ultimately wanted this. She would not have wanted me to suffer continuously."

This courageous woman had single handedly showed me the power of forgiveness not for the sake of others but for the sake of one's own spirit. By forgiving, she released herself from the prison of anger that was ruining her own life.

If she could forgive, what is possible for you?

Soul's Journal Entry #15

Please find a silent place that is comfortable for you and begin answering these questions as honestly as possible. No one but you needs to see this. This is for your spirit and not anyone else's benefit.

Who is it that you need to forgive in your life? What did they do?
_____
_____
_____

What is standing in your way of forgiving them?
_____
_____
_____

How can you alleviate that obstacle? What can you do?
_____
_____
_____

Do you want to forgive them? If not, what are you holding onto by not forgiving them?
_____
_____
_____

What are you losing by not forgiving them?
_____

How is this affecting your health and your life?

How is this affecting your soul?

Would forgiveness benefit you more or them?

Who or what is stopping you from forgiving them?
(If you can't answer this now, then come back to it later.)

CHAPTER SIXTEEN

Be More Conscious of Your Thoughts

*"Life is a mirror and will reflect back
to the thinker what he thinks about."*
~Ernest Holmes

Our thoughts and choices are our most prized possessions. They are the only things in this world that we truly control. They determine our future and quality of life, yet, so many people treat and view their thoughts and choices as just another commodity. They don't respect or recognize their enormous power.

Our thoughts determine who we are and who we will become. Our choices directly impact our destiny. If you believe that your life is for a higher purpose and part of that is finding your passion, then you will find it.

However, if you believe that is for other people and your life is a string of unrelated coincidences, then that is the reality you will create for yourself. It becomes a self-fulfilling prophecy because your brain will constantly look for examples to support your ideas. I call this the "reinforcement loop." What you believe is what your mind will look for in daily life to prove without even being fully aware of it. We all do this on an unconscious level.

If you think you are smart, your mind will look for examples that support this. If you think the opposite, your mind will do the same. You choose your future through your thoughts and actions. They are the only things that are truly yours. Unlike your material possessions that are temporary, your thoughts and choices remain with you and can determine everything.

So why are we so cavalier with our thoughts?

As James Lane Allen so eloquently expressed, "You cannot escape the results of your thoughts…Whatever your present environment may be, you will fall, remain, or rise with your thoughts, visions, and ideals. You will become as small as your controlling desire, as great as your dominant aspiration."

Which do you choose to be?

DISCOVERING YOUR PASSION

Soul's Journal Entry #16

In the past, how have you viewed your thoughts and choices? Have you taken them seriously and made choices that benefit you?
_____
_____
_____

Have your thoughts been a reflection of your values, the values of society, or the values of your family? _____
_____
_____

How has this impacted your life? _____
_____
_____
_____

Do you believe that your choices are your most prized possessions? Why or why not? _____
_____
_____
_____

Has your life been a reflection of this? How? _____
_____
_____
_____

DISCOVERING YOUR PASSION

How have your thoughts and choices affected your life?
_____
_____
_____

Do you try to curb the negative and/or self-defeating thoughts? If yes, how do you do this and does it work?
_____
_____
_____

Are there other strategies that could work better? _____
_____
_____
_____

If changes are made, then how could this impact your life?
_____
_____
_____

CHAPTER SEVENTEEN

Eternal Truths

*In our darkest moments,
the truth can be the light
that illuminates our path forward.*

Some people use their cynicism as a shield. A way to protect themselves from the difficulties of life. Yet, the burden of that cynicism and the lies they carry around can become far more imprisoning than the truth.

We often tell ourselves little white lies as a way of "protecting" ourselves and others. Yet, those little white lies have a way of becoming the truth in some people's mind. A way of hiding the reality behind the mask.

Yet, there are eternal truths that we cannot run away from. These are truths that remain unwavering regardless of their acceptance or realization.

The first truth is that your spirit is eternal and much stronger than you can ever really imagine. In life it is the ordeals that we can't imagine living through that are often forced upon us. Our spirit somehow survives and is much stronger than our mind or body. It is the one factor that keeps us together when everything else is falling apart.

The second eternal truth is that the Universe helps those who help others. Some call this karma. When you help someone, you actually receive more in return. You receive more than they will ever know. The gifts you gain can be beyond measure and often do not fully reveal themselves until months or years later.

This eternal truth became evident one fateful plane ride home. As I boarded the plan to Spokane, Washington I felt broken inside. In many ways, I felt like a failure.

I was not excelling in any area of my life, and often times my whole world felt like a runaway train that was on the path of derailing at any moment. As I boarded the plane, my eyes must have shown my sadness, my body language probably screamed out my internal despair.

On the plane, I began searching for my seat. This took me to the back where I began to settle in for the long ride home. Little did I know this trip would change my life. Little did I know I was sitting next to two parents who had lost their son less than a year ago to a drunk driver. I would have never imagined that they were on the flight to be at the courtroom when the sentence was to be handed down. I had no idea of the pain in their hearts.

I don't remember how the conversation began, yet it was a conversation that I would always remember. I began to talk to about my feelings of confusion and sadness. In a way, I had a captive audience. Where were they going to go?

I began to pour my heart out to two strangers because sometimes it's easier to tell strangers the truth than your own loved ones. I began to talk about my feelings of confusion and sadness. I was clearly living out a path where I felt inadequate and broken inside. The past two years had been the most difficult of my life, and that had left me wondering if I had taken a detour when I should have gone straight. In many ways, I felt lost with despair. I wondered if my life would ever be fair again. Would it ever have the luxury of being easy?

They began to share my sentiments at the often harshness of life. That is when they began to talk about their son, Mark. Mark was a U.S. Ranger. A part of an elite force in the military that jumped out of airplanes and trained in the most adverse combat techniques available. Mark was and always would be their pride and joy. A remarkable man who was just beginning his journey and the path to uncover his own destiny.

Unfortunately, shy of his twenty-third birthday Mark was tragically killed in a car accident. "It will be a year to the date of his death," his Mom would tell me. "That drunk driver who killed him will be sentenced…exactly a year."

Her heart felt a sense of justice amongst the unfairness of it all. A sense that Mark's death would not go unpunished. "She was his friend, and after the accident, instead of helping him she fled the scene. She left him there to die." As she said those words, I could see the pain in her eyes.

During the next hour his parents and I would talk about life's difficulties, the darkness that comes and the reasons it lingers. In their own way, they would make me feel normal for feeling sad, confused, and alone. I would help them understand that they were not alone in the grief for their child. I would talk about my own sister and the life that had been taken so tragically. I spoke of my Mother's experience and the common themes for families that lose a child. I spoke of the immortality that we all share.

"In reality, none of us really dies," I said. "We live on in the lives of those we love. We live on inside of them."

At the end of the flight, Mark's Mom turned to me and said something I will never forget. "By sitting here and talking to us, you have helped two people get through one of the darkest moments of their lives." That day I realized that when we take the time to slow down and bond with others, we are often the ones who get the greatest gift of all. We are the ones who walk away richer and better for it.

That flight was over twenty years ago. I still remember it as if it was yesterday.

That brings us to the final and third eternal truth. This is perhaps the most important one of all. Regardless of what you do or where you go, your destiny finds you. Many people spend a lifetime looking for the right relationship, the right job, the right place to settle down. Yet, in reality when its times for these things or people to come into your life, they will appear. They will find you. Your job is to be the best version of yourself when these things find you.

This is the way of the Universe. It handles the details. You just have to wait, learn, and evolve. No one can do what you do and no one can be you.

DISCOVERING YOUR PASSION

You bring something magical to this world. You touch the lives of others and in many ways, you become the person they need during their darkest hour. You do this for your husband, your wife, your family, friends, and even acquaintances. You become their blessing while they give you the same gift. Don't let cynicism take away your humanity or the parts of you that are special.

No one can be you and that is your superpower. Don't let the hurts of the past or the fear of the future change you because this world needs you. The best version you can give it.

Soul's Journal Entry #17

What are some eternal truths that you have discovered in your own life and through your own unique life experiences?

_____
_____
_____
_____

How have these truths changed you?

_____
_____
_____
_____

What truths have you been hiding from yourself?

_____
_____
_____
_____

What are the white lies you have told yourself and others as a form of "protection?"

DISCOVERING YOUR PASSION

_____
_____
_____
_____

What has been the ultimate cost of white lies? To yourself and to others?

_____
_____
_____
_____

How has it changed you?

_____
_____
_____
_____

What have you learned?

_____
_____
_____
_____

How will your future be different once you are honest with yourself and others?

_____
_____
_____
_____

DISCOVERING YOUR PASSION

Alive

In my frailest hour
I found strength.
In my darkness moments
I searched for hope.

In my burdened soul
I prayed for meaning.
And through this life
I found love.

There have been times when
I have been desperately grief stricken.
And others when I have been elated with joy.

Yet through it all
I have uncovered the beauty
And reverence in living.
The beauty and mystery of life.
For it is grand to be alive.
Truly alive.

DISCOVERING YOUR PASSION

CHAPTER EIGHTEEN

Dream the Impossible Dream

*It is the dreams we imagine unattainable
that our souls feel compelled to chase.*

    I have always wondered what really distinguishes the human race from all other forms. All other species that occupy this vast Earth. Other than our physical and mental attributes, I have always felt that there was something more. Something most people never even think of.

    During one night, due to my inability to sleep, I finally came to an answer. The different between the human species and all other species on this Earth is its ability to envision the impossible dream. To strive to succeed even when the road seems bleak and uphill. To reflect on its own existence with the goal of reaching the truth. Those are what divide the human race from every other race on Earth. That is what makes it so great.

Yet, how many people actually dream the impossible dream? How many even allow themselves the luxury of taking the first step to experience it? How many believe that it can actually come true? How many give up before they have even really tried? The answer is too many.

Most people turn away from their impossible dream consumed with the fear. Yet, the real fear is the possibility of their own internal greatness for it would go against a lifetime of self-limiting beliefs and thoughts. A lifetime of "the truth" turns out to be an illusion.

History is riddled with people who have dreamed the impossible dream and made it a reality. They believed in the power of their own dreams and the possibility that they could come true. They believed that it was in their reach no matter how difficult.

Every one of them had setbacks and disappointments. Every one of them failed at some point and felt broken inside. This is an integral part of the process. Yet, the difference between them and those who abandoned their dreams is their undying determination to never give up. Their unyielding desire to make their dreams a reality. To make their life the dream they wanted to live.

Those who have made an impact are not necessarily smarter, better, or more capable. They just held on when so many before them let go. They looked at adversity for what it truly was – an opportunity to learn and not a punishment.

Of course, they must have had their moments when they felt tired and hopeless inside. Yet, they didn't allow those moments to overtake their spirit. They wouldn't allow it to shatter their soul. Neither should you.

The beauty of dreaming the impossible dream was taught to me by Amanda. An amazing woman whose spirit and courage spoke volumes about her character. At the age of twenty-seven she was diagnosed with multiple sclerosis. A disease that had affected her mother and left her bedridden with despair. She was determined to lead a different life.

On her twenty-eight birthday she began college. A lifelong dream that had been put on the back burner to take care of her ailing mother. She knew her journey would be difficult. Yet, she also knew that she would die with regrets if she didn't try. She set her sights on medical school and worked endlessly to make that dream a reality.

She realized those years of taking care of her mother had given her enormous insights into the lives of people living with chronic health conditions. Insights that her fellow medical students would never have. Insights that could help her save lives.

The day she graduated from medical school was filled with joy and sorrow for her mother had passed away before the graduation. Amanda was and always would be her angel. She would have been so proud to be at the graduation knowing that her daughter didn't give up when so many would have.

Even with her dying mother and her own illness, Amanda taught me the importance of dreaming the impossible dream. In doing so you have no idea who you might reach or touch. You have no idea where your influence will end.

That is the beauty of dreams.

The leave a legacy far greater than we can ever imagine.

DISCOVERING YOUR PASSION

Soul's Journal Entry #18

What is your impossible dream?
_____
_____
_____

What is the biggest obstacle(s) in your way?
_____
_____
_____

What steps can you take to eradicate them?
(This will require brainstorming.)
_____
_____
_____

What can you do today to become one step closer to your dream?
_____
_____
_____

Is your biggest obstacle your own fear of failure?
_____
_____
_____

DISCOVERING YOUR PASSION

On your deathbed, will you regret not trying to achieve that dream?

_____
_____
_____

Is that a risk you are willing to take?

_____
_____
_____

Who do you need to become, what qualities do you need to work on to get closer to your impossible dream?

_____
_____
_____

What can you do today to get closer to that dream?

_____
_____
_____

Create an *Action Plan* that will give you a roadmap to achieving your dream. What does that look like for you? Make it as detailed as you want.

_____
_____
_____

DISCOVERING YOUR PASSION

CHAPTER NINETEEN

Actions

*Life humbles you as you age.
You finally realize how much time
was wasted on nonsense.*

At your funeral no one will praise you for putting in the most time at work. No one will remember your accomplishments, but they will remember your actions. How you treated those who had no influence on your life. Those who could neither harm nor help you. For that is the truest test of a human being.

My Mother would always tell me when I was growing up that when we leave this Earth all that remains are our actions because they are eternal. They are the only things that are truly ours. They will follow us into the afterlife and they will be what we are remembered for. Everything else will disappear.

Our job will be taken over by a stranger. Our house will have new occupants. The material possessions that we hold in such high esteem will be given to others. The only thing that is eternal are our actions – good or bad. They follow us when everything else fades away.

It takes some a lifetime to realize their material possessions never really belong to them. They are given in the form of a loan while on Earth. We become guardians of the things we are given or earn. This expires the day we die. It is non-negotiable. There are no second changes.

Throughout my life, my wise and insightful Mother always emphasized the importance of personal actions and choices. She believed that actions determined a person's path through life. They could either become an individual's greatest asset or liability in life. They determined the difference between a life of abundance and one of misery. "A foolish action or decision today can affect your life for decades to come," was my paternal grandmother's favorite expression in Farsi. It was something she was known for repeating over and over again.

My Mom agreed with her and would often repeat the same words to my brother, Thatcher, and I while we were growing up. She believed that every choice or decision either brought a person closer to or further away from their true path. From the life they had always wanted. She believed that one wrong step off the path could affect every other step moving forward. In her mind, those crooked steps represented poor choices or actions. "Every person strives for a better life, yet how many actually make decisions that foster the creation of one?" she expressed often.

She would point to the person who desired financial security yet spent hours at the mall shopping. Or the person who wanted a committed relationship yet remained locked up in his/her home staring at their phone night after night. She would go on to mention many others who actions and desires did not synchronize together, then she would begin to talk about the repercussions.

In her lifetime of wisdom, my Mother would also talk about the most destructive of all actions. The physical manifestation of anger. This has ruined more lives and relationships than any other action or emotion on Earth. In a fit of anger, rational decision making virtually disappears.

So the next time you are about to become angry and express harsh words stop for a moment and ask yourself, "Is this how I want to be remembered? Is this going to be my legacy?" And then start again. That is the beauty of life…you can always start again. That is until the day you die. Then the loan expires and another chapter begins. A new type of journey ensues.

DISCOVERING YOUR PASSION

Soul's Journal Entry #19

What actions in the past have you regretted?
_____
_____
_____

What type of mark have they left on yourself and others?
_____
_____
_____

How can you rectify this?
_____
_____
_____

What can you do to make sure this pattern of behavior does not continue?
_____
_____
_____

How will that change your life?
_____
_____
_____

DISCOVERING YOUR PASSION

How will that change your legacy?

_____
_____
_____

How do you want to be remembered?

_____
_____
_____

Cleansing the Soul

Every day we cleanse our body.
Yet, do we ever really cleanse our soul?
Cleanse it from the everyday burdens of life,
The struggles, the setbacks,
The disappointments and the pain.

The truth is everybody has a story to tell.
A story of love, loss, and betrayal.
A story that haunts them.
A story that can weigh down their heart
And harden their soul.

Yet, we were not given life to be burdened by
The stories that befall us.
Or the stories that we tell ourselves.
We were given life to love, learn, and evolve.
We were given life to live.

So the next time you find yourself burdened
By the stories of life
Consider cleaning your soul
By writing your true feelings
Without anyone else ever seeing it.

It may help unburden your spirit
From the stories that we tell ourselves.
From the stories that keep us imprisoned
In a past that doesn't exist anymore.
A past that only lives on in our minds.

CHAPTER TWENTY

Draining Your Soul

*Better to admit that you walked
through the wrong door
then spend a lifetime in the wrong room.*

We all have those days that feel as if they've lasted a lifetime. Days that seem to never really end. Days that we wish would never come again. These days drain our soul. Yet, it is not only these days, it's also the little troubles that can add up and completely deplete our energy leaving us barren inside.

Another important step in finding your passion is to ask yourself what is draining your soul? Is it the clutter in your home? The jobs that never get done around the house? The people who leave you with negativity and doubts? The relationship that's going nowhere? Or the job where you feel completely unappreciated and overburdened? Which one of these are depleting your energy? Which one of these is draining your soul?

Often times, to the outside world, we may look like we are succeeding maybe even thriving, yet, internally we feel depleted in so many different ways.

To find your passion, you need to realize the outside forces that are draining your spirit, and begin to design a plan to eradicate them so you can start feeling whole inside.

This became even more apparent when I met Dorothy. Dororthy was a sixty-two-year-old school teacher who felt depleted in so many ways. Her job was incredibly demanding, her home was very unorganized and filled with clutter, her friends were endlessly talking about the difficulties of growing older. At times, she felt that her soul was drowning.

When I met Dorothy, we began to discuss the factors that were leading to her internal dilemmas. The outside influences that were completely draining her energies. Initially she thought fibromyalgia was to blame. She was constantly tired and ridden with aches and pains and horrible migraines. "Could these health problems be a direct consequence of your life? Could they be telling you something?" I would gently ask.

During the next several weeks Dorothy began a complete overhaul of her life. She began to get rid of the clutter in her home, gain control of her classroom again, and stop talking with her negative and toxic friends. She began to take control of her life. Instead of being a passive passenger, she was ready to take the wheel. She realized a life of default is often a life of quiet desperation.

This new version began to take care of herself. She joined yoga and began to take bubble baths every night. Just these two changes made her feel better. She started to eat healthier and made sure her body received proper nutrients. She began to exercise.

Within a matter of four week her life and attitude completely changed. She no longer accepted other people's toxic energy and their baggage. She no longer felt that her life was draining her soul. For the first time in a long time, she felt in control. She began to live again. And once these changes were made, she refused to go back to her old life and her toxic family and friends that drained her soul instead of feeding it.

DISCOVERING YOUR PASSION

Soul's Journal Entry #20

Make a list of all the factors/things/people in your life that are draining your spirit.

_____
_____
_____

How is this affecting your emotional and physical health?

_____
_____
_____

How is this impacting your relationships?

_____
_____
_____

What can you do to begin alleviating that today?

_____
_____
_____

How would your life change?

_____
_____
_____

DISCOVERING YOUR PASSION

What is stopping you?

_____
_____
_____

CHAPTER TWENTY-ONE

I'm the Problem

Wherever you go
there you are.
There is no escaping yourself.

In 2022, Taylor Swift released the song "Anti-Hero" from her 10th studio album "Midnights." She iconically sings in the song, "It's me. Hi, I'm the problem, it's me." This song became an anthem for women everywhere who were willing to look in the mirror and be brutally honest with themselves. And I will admit, I was one of them. Let me explain.

For as long as I can remember, I never really *allowed* myself to enjoy life. When one goal was met, I was quickly moving onto the next goal never taking the time to just sit back and celebrate my small accomplishments.

Don't get me wrong, there were fleeting moments of happiness, yet, they soon would be overtaken with thoughts of what I needed to do next, potential problems that could pop up, things I needed to overcome, and struggles I was still ruminating on. I would allow these negative thoughts to take over my soul and leave me disillusioned with life.

It wasn't until a conversation with my Father that I began to realize that I was the problem. The common denominator was always me.

It was the summer of 2001. I had just come back from Salt Lake City to spend the summer with my parents. My Father and I had been spending time together when he said those fateful words that altered my perspective. I am sure he had said such words many times before, yet for some reason they began to sink in that summer. A day I still remember vividly. The conversation started off in a very amusing manner. My parents had prided themselves on the beauty their backyard. To help you understand how magnificent it was here is a picture. Yet, for the past year, that beautiful yard had been plagued with a disease that had left their once velvet lawn patchy, yellow, and brittle. My Father would point to the best part of the

lawn (that was still thriving) and tell my Mom, "Look how beautiful it looks today?" Her response was often filled with laughter. She wondered why he would ignore the rest of the yard and only concentrate on the one patch that seemed to have avoided the disease.

On cue, he would then raise his hand and say, "That is the secret of life. Instead of focusing on the negativity, one should realize the beauty that still existed. For the beauty is far more relevant and revealing."

He would also share with me later:

> In life, two people may look at the same waterfall. One may see the danger and force behind that natural occurrence. The other sees the beauty and mystery of the water. Instead of being that person who focuses on the danger, be the individual who appreciates the beauty. The beauty is all around us, but often we are too busy to notice it.

He went on to explain that most individuals never really enjoy their lives because they were too busy focusing on what they don't have instead of the gifts that are right in front of them. (Sadly, I was one of those people for many years.) It's only when they lose those gifts do they realize how valuable they were.

He believed that happiness was not about wanting or having more, it was about wanting what you already had. It was about being aware of even the smallest blessings.

Considering the life my Father had experienced it was amazing he had such a positive outlook. At the young age of 12, he witnessed the death of his own Dad. Then years later the death of his 19-year-old (first-born) daughter in a car accident. And then the loss of his homeland in a revolution which forced him to start over in his late 50's in a foreign country, with a foreign language, and a culture he didn't understand.

Any one of those events would make a person bitter, yet he refused to allow that. He knew that it wasn't what happened to him that mattered the most – it was his reaction. That day I realized why his soul was still young at heart even after a lifetime of heartaches and disappointments. He always looked for the positive even in a difficult situation.

Coming home from a hard day, he would repeatedly tell me, "If there were 10 things I wanted to accomplish today and I only reached 5 of my goals then I focus on the 5 that were successful. I focus on what I got right every single time."

It took me many years to finally understand what he was trying to tell me all along. I understood the gift he had given me.

If you focus on what you don't have, you will never have enough.

If you focus on what you do have, then you will always have too much.

Your life is determined by what you focus. Not what happens to you.

DISCOVERING YOUR PASSION

Soul's Journal Entry #21

Make a list of all the things you are grateful for.
_____
_____
_____
_____
_____

How often are you thankful for all your blessings?
_____

How often do you feel a person should be thankful for their blessings? In other words, how often should they express their gratitude for what they have (even to themselves).
_____
_____

Do you do this? Are you thankful that often?
_____

How has this affected your life?
_____
_____

Are you willing to be more grateful for your blessings? What about staring a journal where you write down five things you are grateful for every day? They can be as small as the ability to breath easily to spending time with your favorite person or pet.
_____

DISCOVERING YOUR PASSION

Are you willing to be more reflective on your blessings? _____

How could that change your life?
_____
_____
_____

Have you ever wondered how some people who go through horrible heartaches can come out grateful, yet some who are given everything in life remain ungrateful? Why do you think that is?
_____
_____
_____

DISCOVERING YOUR PASSION

Success

What is success?
The expensive car in the driveway?
The house by the sea?
The fancy degree on the wall?

People scramble and sacrifice their mental and physical health
Every day to achieve material success in this world.
Yet, do they ever really enjoy it?

To understand true success,
One must judge their accomplishments
Not by what they gained
But by what they had to give up
In order to gain them.

Real success is looking into the eyes of your child
And realizing that you have given up more
So they would not live with less.

Success is understanding that your job does not define you.
It is an opportunity to make a difference,
Regardless of what you actually do.

Succes is finding meaning in your life
And peace in your soul

DISCOVERING YOUR PASSION

Success is never missing a recital, play, or game
For they grow up so fast
And remember those moments with you
More than they remember the toys.

Success is looking into your spouse's eyes
And realizing that you love them
More than you need them.

Success is kissing your child goodnight
And making sure a day does not go by
That they don't hear you say
"I love you."

Success is knowing that you have
Touched another person's life without
Them ever knowing who you are.

For the act is far more important than their gratitude.
That is all true success.

DISCOVERING YOUR PASSION

CHAPTER TWENTY-TWO

Who is Stopping You?

*The greatest failure is not in losing the battle
it's in failing to even try to win the war.*

Looking back on my life, I have realized that every individual I have ever met revealed an inner desire to do something more. This ranged from going back to school, taking art classes, or starting an epic adventure or business. Yet, for external reasons they too often decide against it.

These encounters have taught me that our biggest barriers or limitations are often ourselves. We are the ones who stand in our own way. I know a little about this because I am completely guilty of it.

When I close my eyes, I can vividly remember being in my high school counselor's office as a senior. His name was Mr. McCray. He was a wonderful man with a deep laugh and a full beard.

"What are your dreams?" he asked me one afternoon while sitting in his office. I started to give him a list of all the things I would like to accomplish. Ending the short monologue with "I'm not sure I can do all of it or really any of it." He turned to me in a very serious tone and said words I would carry with me forever.

"The world will try to limit you, there is no need for you to do it to yourself." Twenty years later I still remember the look in his eyes when he shared those words with me. For a moment, there was silence in the room as I allowed his words to really sink in. That was a day I will never forget. That image and his words come back to me often when I am trying to convince myself that something is out of my reach.

In life, we often tell ourselves that we are not good enough, smart enough, or talented. Sadly, the more we repeat those words the more we believe them.

Throughout my life, I have been blessed with wonderful friends starting in high school. Some I still talk to and some that I haven't seen in years but still remain close to my heart. One of those friends was Sarah.

Sarah and I would spend hours talking about our mutual love for writing and creating something out of nothing. We both hoped to become published authors one day. To share our words with the world in hope that it would provide some comfort or reprieve from life's challenges.

Yet, with all the brilliance and talent that my friend possessed the one thing she didn't possess was a belief in herself. It was these conversations with Sarah that I realized how we all have one thing in common. Most of us struggle to really believe in ourselves. We believe in others, but often we lack that same sentiment towards ourselves. We convince ourselves we are defeated before even beginning. Yet, this robs us of using our skills and talents and those who may benefit from them.

For example, my life has been greatly enriched by people who strove for their dreams even if it was a long shot. They wrote books, made movies, took on challenges knowing that failure was possible *but not the only possibility*. My life has been enriched by their unwillingness to give up.

My greatest hope for the person reading this is you realize your strengths before believing in your limitations. For your contribution to the world would be missed. This is the saddest of all occurrences – not success or failure – but the failure to even try. That has killed more dreams than failure ever could.

So, what is stopping you?

DISCOVERING YOUR PASSION

Soul's Journal Entry #22

What are some of your dreams? Be as specific as possible.

_____
_____
_____

Are you stopping yourself from even trying? If yes, then why?

_____
_____
_____

Who or what is really stopping you? And are they real limitations or limitations you have convinced yourself of?

_____
_____
_____

What can you do today to start overcoming these challenges?

_____
_____
_____

How would your life change if you started trying?

_____
_____
_____

CHAPTER TWENTY-THREE

Trust

In our darkest hours all we have is faith.
All we need is trust, all we can do is pray.
For no matter what befalls us or
the stories we tell ourselves,
a new day with come, a ray of hope will emerge
that leads us from the darkness into the light again.

Often times the first quality to be lost in life is trust. Trust in ourselves and trust in those around us. Throughout the years, as we become hurt by others, trust is the first quality to disappear. Yet, in reality it is the one quality we need the most.

DISCOVERING YOUR PASSION

How can you ever find your passion in life when you don't trust yourself, your intuition, or the experiences and people who come into your life? No one is more worthy of your trust than yourself. No one is more deserving.

The first way to regain your trust is to begin believing in your power again. Your power to overcome the dark nights and bounce back smarter and better than before. Most people don't understand or even think about the unexpected gifts that problems and challenges can provide. They force us to rise to the occasion. They force the best out of us.

The first way to regain your trust is to start believing in yourself again. To go back to that fearless boy or girl that you were growing up.

"Yet how can I trust myself when no one else seems to believe in me?" Hazel expressed loudly one cloudy afternoon. Hazel's Mom was a superstar in her industry. Someone who people admired and respected. "There is no way I can ever reach her level of admiration from others. When I'm with her, I often feel invisible."

I looked at her and said, "Why would you want to repeat what your Mother has accomplished? You have gifts that others would kill for, but you are so caught up in comparing yourself to your Mother than you almost lose sight of the enormous innate talent that you have been given."

For a moment, that made her reflect. She went on to explain how her family had disapproved of all her decisions. Her decision on who to marry, where to work, and ultimately where to live. She felt like a failure in their eyes. As a result, she began to completely lose trust in herself. Her confidence began to erode and it started to impact her marriage.

"Are you happy?" I would ask. She looked at me with a blank look in her eyes as if no one had ever bothered to ask. "Are you happy?" I repeated myself.

"Well, yes, but that's not the point," she replied.

I would go on to explain that no matter what they believed it was ultimately her journey to follow. Their disapproval was born out of their inability to understand. To understand her. They would never know how it felt to be her. How it felt to live through her eyes. And in many ways, they never could.

"Throughout our life there will be times when we all make mistakes. This shouldn't affect our ability to believe in ourselves. Even as we make mistakes, they teach us more than our greatest successes. They have a bigger role in who we become and how we connect to others," I said.

Regardless of what the outside world believes, you should always trust and believe in yourself. At the end of the day, only you can save yourself. Other people's opinions are just that – what they think. It doesn't make it fact.

Trust the gifts you've been given. They are there for a reason. It all serves a bigger purpose that you can't see now. Begin to search for that purpose, for those activities that fill your soul, and you will find your passion.

It's been there all along. Buried under other people's expectations and society's opinions, waiting to be released. Don't betray yourself by letting them stay buried. You deserve to know your value, and this world needs your gifts.

Doing the work, creating the art – that is success no matter what anyone else thinks. I believe in you. Start now, start today, but please just start.

DISCOVERING YOUR PASSION

Soul's Journal Entry #23

Do you believe in yourself? Do you believe in your intuition? If no, what are examples in your past that showed you that this was a mistake? Provide as many examples as possible. _____
_____
_____
_____
_____

If someone you loved did not trust themselves, their own abilities, their own strength, then what type of advice would you give to them? What would you say to them? _____
_____
_____
_____

If you started believing in yourself today, how would that change your life? How would that change you? _____
_____
_____
_____

How has not believing in yourself affected your life, the way you view yourself, and your relationships with others? _____
_____
_____
_____

DISCOVERING YOUR PASSION

What Would You Do?

What would you do
If you could not fail?
If doing the work was the prize?
If walking away was a betrayal of self?

Climb a mountain?
Sail the sea?
Run a marathon?
Finally be free?

Free of everyday burdens, struggles, and pain.
Free of your own internal chains.
For they hold you back more than you'll ever know.
Never really allowing you to grow.

A lifetime is spent
Chasing the dreams of strangers
All in the hope of avoiding any dangers.

Yet, what is the purpose
Of a life spent for others?
When all you really wanted
Was some peace and comfort.

Ask yourself once,
"What would I do if I could not fail?
What if just creating equaled success?
What if walking away was a betrayal to self?"

You'll be surprised at how your life changes
Once you realize the only person
You really need to impress is
The person staring right back at you.

DISCOVERING YOUR PASSION

CHAPTER TWENTY-FOUR

What if You Could Not Fail?

Are you more afraid of failure or
the disapproval of others?
Are you more afraid of your inherent weakness?
or the chance that you are stronger
than you could ever really imagine?
What are you really afraid of?

Many people dream of being famous. What I think they are really dreaming of *is to be seen*. To be seen for their most authentic self. To be seen for who they really are. And not in what the world has told them to be. And somehow this is confused with "fame."

DISCOVERING YOUR PASSION

At some point in everyone's life, each person needs to ask themselves this series of questions:

What would I do if I knew in my heart that I could not fail? If I knew that creating what was in my soul, the truest expression of myself, was the prize?

If the success was inherent in doing the work?

These questions, if answered honestly, have the extraordinary ability to change lives.

What would you do if you could not fail?

What dreams would you follow?

What risks would you be willing to take?

These are the questions some never ask themselves. Not because the answers are hard. They fail to answer them because they know it could rock their world. They are afraid it would force them to make drastic changes, but that can be furthest from the truth.

The key in discovering your passion is not to quit your dependable day job and tour the world singing. Or to sell everything and start an art gallery.

The key to discovering your passion is to begin doing that passion while living your normal life. Let's be honest, most of us won't reach the level of success like Taylor Swift, Tom Cruise, or Jennifer Lopez. Yet, each of us has things we can do every day that nourish our spirit. That make us feel excited to be alive again. That bring gratitude into our lives by doing – not just being.

To be completely honest, for a long time I was afraid to ask myself those questions. Afraid of what the answers would reveal about me and my inability to display courage when I really needed it most. I judged myself for not following what I really wanted and instead falling prey to what I thought the world wanted.

This all ended when I met Barbara. She was one of those ladies whose is a triple threat – smart, successful, and savvy. On the outside, she had it all. What could she possibly be sad about?

Barbara was thirty-five years old timeless beauty, yet her eyes revealed an internal bitterness and resentment towards life. One day after a few drinks, she revealed things that surprised me.

"My whole life has been decided for me. From the moment I was born, I had a family who told me who I would be. My parents made all my decisions from how I should act, what kind of career I could have and what kind of man was 'appropriate' to marry. Do you know that I didn't even pick my own wedding date? It was picked by my family because more people could attend?" she said.

For a moment, I was stunned. I couldn't believe what she was revealing after all the years we had known each other. On the outside, she had it all. Yet, anyone could see the bitterness edged into her wrinkles.

"Was it all a mistake?" I asked.

"No, of course not," she responded immediately.

"So what would you do if you could not fail?"

It took several minutes for her to respond, as if no one had ever bothered to ask this question. "If I knew I could not fail, I would start singing again." she shared. "Singing makes me feel free, it makes me feel like I've accomplished something. Created something no one else could create. When I write songs, I get excited about the process," she shared.

I smiled and replied, "Why don't you do that now?"

She looked at me dumfounded.

"You create music because it's what our soul is called to do. The material success of that is out of your hands. Your job is to create and by doing that you inspire others. There is something magical in just creating something that never existed before. It doesn't have to be listened to by a million people. It only has to be listened by you. And now with technology you can put it online, and if it improves someone's day by listening to it, then that is a topping but not the sole reason to create."

"You create because you have it. Because your soul needs to express itself in the way *it* sees fit. Because creating is the success. Having the courage to express yourself is the reward. Van Gogh was Van Gogh before anyone knew him. He became famous after he died but that didn't mean he wasn't an artistic genius while he was alive. You create because you have to. It's your rent for living in this world."

I think the most important lesson I learned from that conversation is that no one, not your family, friends, teaches or even your therapist can protect you from your suffering. You can't cry it away or punch it away or drink it away. You can't shop it away or even exercise it away. Suffering is a part of the human experience. And all the distractions, alcohol, drugs, toys, success try to numb or decrease the suffering.

As we move through life and gain wisdom we learn how to survive and thrive in spite of the suffering. And if we are really lucky and have the opportunity to help someone else then it gives meaning to our pain. All we can hope is to move on and become better because of the suffering. One way we can move on constructively is to create. Create art, create writing, create something from nothing because that is what our soul is screaming to do. To create and be seen.

She smiled at me. I think she was surprised by my response, but the moment I was done I saw a glimmer in her eyes. An excitement that hadn't been there before.

I am proud to say that my friend Barbara started to sing again. Her voice was and is a gift to anyone who hears it. She shares her songs online and has found a community of like-minded people. More importantly, it has revitalized her and brought joy to her life. Ultimately, that is the whole point of discovering our passions. It's the art that saves us by giving us a reprieve from life's rollercoaster. That is independent of success.

And one day if we are lucky, we realize that the action of creating is the success. It creates space to be authentically real in the way that nothing else can. And that is when we are really seen.

DISCOVERING YOUR PASSION

Soul's Journal Entry #24

What would you do if you could not fail? What dreams would you follow? What risks would you take? _____
_____
_____
_____
_____

How would your actions leading to it be different from what they are now? _____
_____
_____
_____

How would you need to change or do to accomplish this? _____
_____
_____
_____
_____

What are some resources you can use at your disposal?
_____
_____
_____

Who are the people in your life that could help you?

DISCOVERING YOUR PASSION

Who are the people in your life that stand in the way?

Why are they still in your life?

What could you do to decrease their toxic contribution?

How would your life change?

DISCOVERING YOUR PASSION

CHAPTER TWENTY-FIVE

Secret Dreams

*Some secret dreams are so grand
that even the prospect of failure
can never erase them.*

We all have them. I call them secret dreams. Dreams that we don't share with anyone for fear of being judged or worse yet criticized for just having them. "How can you dream that? It's so out of reach."

These are dreams that we think about in the solitude of our own life. Dreams that some take with them to their grave. Even the closest people in their lives may never know of their secret dreams. They are never shared for a variety of reasons. Some may never divulge them because of fear.

DISCOVERING YOUR PASSION

Yet, somewhere in our hearts we know that's not the complete truth. In reality, we don't tell people because we fear that we could actually do it, but that would mean rearranging our whole life, coming out of our comfort zone, possibly even changing careers.

It would force us to make hard decisions. And what if we fail? The truth is that you will never know until you try. Often times, the first step, telling someone, opening up can be the hardest. Don't worry about failure, worry about the chances you miss when you don't even try.

There will always be a reason to keep your secret dreams inside, but by doing that you betray yourself. You betray the parts of yourself that need to be seen.

I started writing this book over twenty years ago. At a time when others believed it was a waste of my time. I had other obligations and responsibilities to think about. I was fully aware of their points, yet inside of me this book was just waiting to come out.

My reason for writing this book was to help others on the path to find their dreams. To find the activities that brought them joy in life, that made them feel alive, that made waking up each morning a blessing and not a burden.

The one piece of wisdom that I think is essential is to never discourage someone else's dream. No matter how unrealistic it seems or out of reach, it is their dream. And by discouraging them you are doing them the biggest disservice.

Now should everyone quit their job and chase their dreams – not necessarily. You can still pursue your dream when you are not at work. The reality is that we all need to work. We all need to find a way to pay the bills and if you can do that while still pursing the activities that make you feel alive – then you have found a middle ground that can save you. Save you from the monotony of life.

Because life can feel like a grind. Get up, go to work, come home, sleep and repeat.

To counter the repetition of life we all need hobbies, activities, something that gives us something to look forward to. A reason to get up in the morning.

I pray that I will finally finish this book even twenty years later. I pray that it will have an impact on someone's life. I pray that those who discourage dreams will realize their mistakes. You may never know how much it means to them. Just because it is not your dream doesn't mean it's not worthy of their time. It may be the one thing that saves them.

<u>Soul's Journal Entry #25</u>

What are your secret dreams?

_____
_____
_____

Why have you not shared them with others?

_____
_____
_____

Who do you really trust?

_____
_____
_____

What do you really fear? (Is the actual failure greater than the fear of it?)

DISCOVERING YOUR PASSION

_____
_____
_____

It is justified? How can you overcome it? What are steps you can start today.

_____
_____
_____

The best time to start on your dream is yesterday. The second-best time is now. So what are you waiting for?

_____
_____
_____

CHAPTER TWENTY-SIX

Unlimited Resources

*Each human soul is a wealth of resources,
a fountain of knowledge,
a library of wisdom.
It possesses an inherent beauty
that can't be erased with time.*

What would you do if money was not a factor in your life? If you could have complete disregard of the finances or expenses in pursuing your passion? How would your life be different from the one you lead today?

That is what I call the dream of unlimited resources. The life they would lead if money, time, and other people's opinions were not a factor. Yet, realistically this is all in our reach. If we are given barriers, we are also given a doorway out. If we are given limitations, we are also granted choices. Choices that can mitigate the present situation.

Yet, sadly instead of focusing on these choices, most individuals focus on the reasons their dreams are unattainable. The qualities they don't possess. The obstacles in their way. If people took a fraction of the time focused on negativity and instead focus on the solutions, then it is amazing what can be done. It is amazing how far they would go.

If you believe that your dreams are out of reach and that you will never find and pursue your passion, then that is exactly what will occur. It becomes a self-fulfilling prophecy. At the end of the day, the difference between the person who lives his/her dreams and the one who wonders about it is courage. The courage to face adversity and challenges with the perseverance of a fighter. The courage to continue the fight when the road is uphill and windy. The courage to stand up to challenges when they seem overwhelming. The courage to try again even if it's against the odds.

In my mind the story of Hellen Keller has always been the epitome of unlimited resources. Even though she faced the world as a blind and mute woman. Hellen Keller did more in one lifetime that many with healthy bodies and IQ's well over 150. She did not focus on her limitations. Instead, she focused on the unlimited resources within herself. She focused on her strengths instead of her disabilities. She focused on her dreams.

The story of Abraham Lincoln also represents another prime example of a human soul who focused on his inner abilities rather his external failures. He practically failed in everything that he

DISCOVERING YOUR PASSION

attempted. He failed to get into law school. He failed as a businessman (twice). He failed numerous attempts to become a city representative, a senator, and even vice-president. He experienced a nervous breakdown which kept him in bed for six months. And to make it even worse his fiancé died shortly before their wedding.

It is amazing that one of the greatest presidents of all time was actually considered a failure for most of his life.

And of course, we all know the amazing story of Michael Jordan. Perhaps, the greatest basketball player of all time. Yet, how many of you were aware that he did not make the cut for his high school basketball team his junior year? Now isn't that amazing? Just imagine what you could accomplish if you focused on the resources within you instead of the limitations out there.

Soul's Journal Entry #26

Make a list of all your internal resources or characteristics that can help change your life?

_____
_____
_____

Which one of these do you not use?

_____
_____
_____

How has this impacted your life?

_____
_____
_____

DISCOVERING YOUR PASSION

Do you allow obstacles to discourage you from even trying?
_____
_____

Do you give up easily? Why?
_____
_____

What can you do to prevent this in the future?
_____
_____

What is stopping you?
_____
_____

CHAPTER TWENTY-SEVEN

The Others

*Coming to the end of their life
only to realize that they have never really lived,
never really chased their dreams
that is one of the greatest losses of all.*

At different points in our life, we watch others live out our dreams. We witness them achieve the goals we wanted for ourselves. We see them fulfill our aspirations, and in the process, we watch and learn. Then in the darkness, by ourselves, we wonder what they possess that is lacking in us.

What makes them different?

Why are they so special?

The answer is they are not. They are not smarter, or better, or even more talented. They just had the will to chase their dreams and not let anything stand in their way.

I call them "the others." We often see them on our journey. Somethings they pass us by. Other times we see them at a distance. Yet, each time we wonder about their inner qualities. Their inner characteristics that make them so different.

Sadly, it can take a lifetime of experiences and mistakes to realize the only difference between them and us is fear. Fear of failure, fear of the unknown, fear of disappointment, maybe even fear of realizing the enormous ability within ourselves that remains hidden for that would go against a lifetime of self-defeating thoughts and beliefs.

Every human emotion or decision comes from one of two places – fear or love. These are the greatest driving forces of the human psyche. They explain our behavior. They build the foundation of all other emotions.

You can't just love to sing – you have to love the process. For the process is where all the work is done. All the endless nights and rewrites. The only difference between those who live out their dreams and those who help others achieve theirs is the fear of failure and the love of the process.

Fear can paralyze more people internally than any setback, disappointment, or struggle. It destroys more dreams and passions than any force on Earth. It is the main reason people fail to live their best life possible. It is the main cause for most human unhappiness.

This life lesson was driven home the day I met Nicole. Nicole was a beautiful thirty-two-year-old doctor. She was married to a prominent surgeon and enjoyed all the finer things in life. Yet, she was always afraid. Fearful that something bad would happen. Fearful that her world would suddenly be turned upside down. Afraid that she would lose everything. At times that fear was paralyzing.

Her ultimate dream was to lead a happy and quiet life. Yet, her fear was not allowing her to even enjoy everyday pleasures. She was constantly in a state of anxiety and sadness. "I felt so blessed in life that somewhere in the back of my mind I thought it would all soon end. That my children would be hurt, my marriage would fall apart, or that I would lose my job."

Her fear that it would all come to an end got in the way of appreciating what had been given to her. She would often watch others who seemed to be struggling or with greater problems be so much happier than her. Where she felt as if she was drowning, they seemed to be thriving. On the outside she seemed to have it all. On the inside, it was very much the opposite.

We would spend hours talking about the power of fear. It's power to rob people of their dreams, their destiny, their sanity, their peace of mind. "What are you willing to do in order to break free of this?" I would ask her. "What can I do?" she would reply immediately. "At times it feels so overwhelming. At times I feel that the fear has more control over me than I have control over it."

After some point Nicole began to clearly see the impact fear was having on her life. It was robbing her of the ability to feel gratitude, to express love, and to ultimately live. It was robbing her of the dream of a quiet and joyful life. It was robbing her of everything she had ever wanted. She realized that the fear was unfounded. It was a consequence of her irrational thoughts and unwarranted beliefs.

When I would meet Nicole again three months later, she seemed different. She had been seeing a therapist. There was a sparkle in her eyes that had been previously missing. A joy in her voice that seemed lost. She explained that by conquering her irrational fears and recognizing them for what they were, she had finally regained control of her life.

She began to live again.

<u>Soul's Journal Entry #27</u>

What are your fears?
_____
_____
_____

How are they affecting your life?
_____
_____
_____

How are they affecting your relationship with yourself, your spouse, or children?
_____
_____
_____

How are they controlling your life and actions?
_____
_____
_____

DISCOVERING YOUR PASSION

Are they based on irrational thoughts and beliefs. (Take a moment before answering this one to really ponder the true meaning.) If yes, what are those beliefs? Where have they come from?

_____
_____
_____

What are the steps necessary to eradicate them from your life?

_____
_____
_____

How will your life change?

_____
_____
_____

DISCOVERING YOUR PASSION

CHAPTER TWENTY-SEVEN

Ten Steps Closer to Your Dreams

A Formula for Success

Many years ago, I realized that success like failure has a formula. There are steps each of us can take to increase our chances for success. The steps below are not exhaustive. Please add your own steps from your own life experiences. And if you think this may help someone – please share these steps with them.

You never know how your words can impact someone. It can literally mean the difference between never trying and finally giving themselves a chance. Ultimately the worse betrayal in life doesn't come from our romantic partners – it comes from betraying ourselves and the lives we could have led.

DISCOVERING YOUR PASSION

THE TEN STEPS TO ACHIEVING YOUR DREAMS

STEP 1   BELIEVE and IMAGINE

The first step in achieving your dreams is to believe in their possibility. To believe in a future that incorporates your dreams, and then imagine yourself doing it. There is a self-fulfilling prophecy that happens when we imagine our dreams over and over again. Some say this works because our vibrational frequency changes thereby aligning with those action. Others say that when you make visions in your mind it translates into realities in your life.

BELIEVE and IMAGINE until it becomes second nature to you.

STEP 2   BECOME AN EXPERT

Learn as much as you possibly can about the dream. What is the process? What are the resources that will help you? There are patterns to success just like there are patterns to failure. Make sure you know what those are. Talk to people who have already achieved what you want to do. The internet has become a valuable resource for this because of social media. Do your research and find people. If you write a sincere letter or e-mail about your dreams and your unyielding desire, most people will be more than willing to offer some advice or valuable direction. The key is to remain consistent, honest, and sincere.

STEP 3   DESIGN A PLAN

As my wise older brother, Thatcher, would tell me growing up, no ship has ever made it to the harbor with a plan. No dream has ever come true without a blueprint. You will absolutely need a plan. Make it as detailed as possible. Write it down and make your ideas and intentions clear. Then the pieces of the puzzle will begin to fall into place.

STEP 4   NOTHING WILL SUBSTITUTE HARD WORK

The realization of any passion or dream requires a tremendous amount of hard work. It requires the postponement of instant gratification for the reality of a far greater gift in return. Be willing to work incredibly hard. There are no shortcuts to anything worth having.

STEP 5   GO WITH THE FLOW

There will always be unexpected occurrences on your journey to achieve your goals. Yet, by learning from them instead of letting them discourage you, they serve as a tool to make your dreams more attainable. Every "no" is one step closer to a "yes." Remember some of the most accomplished people also faced the greatest obstacles and failures. The difference is that they learned from them and instead of a stumbling block they became a stepping stone.

STEP 6   SURROUND YOURSELF WITH SUPPORT

This will be your saving grace during the setbacks and defeats. As my wise Father would always say, "Every setback or defeat is a lesson in disguise." Never underestimate the enormous power of having a good support network that can celebrate your small and big wins along with giving you encouragement when the road becomes challenging. If you do not learn from the lessons behind these situations, then they will reappear in another area of your life.

STEP 7   HAVE PATIENCE

Time is on your side when it comes to achieving goals. Whenever you feel that your dreams are out of reach, take a break, recharge, and regroup but don't give up. These are tests to reveal your true conviction. How bad do you really want it?

DISCOVERING YOUR PASSION

STEP 8   BRAINSTORM, BRAINSTORM, BRAINSTORM

Anytime you get in a difficult situation or have an obstacle in your way, the more you brainstorm the greater the outcome. Don't think outside the box, think as if there is no box. That mantra will take you far.

STEP 9   ELIMINATE THE OBSTACLES

The best way to eliminate obstacles is to go right through them. Every obstacle has a solution. Just because you can't imagine it now doesn't mean the solution is not out there. Brainstorming, creating a plan, and having patience are the three most critical elements when it comes to eliminating obstacles.

STEP 10   GIVE YOUR TIME TO OTHERS

There was a period of my life that I was constantly volunteering when I had free time. I volunteered for drives, initiatives, fundraisers, anything that I could get my hands on. The most surprising thing happened when I helped others - it put my own problems into perspective. What I had imagined as a huge dilemma became much more manageable when I used some time to help someone else and get outside of my own head. There is something magical about helping others, volunteering, or working with your church. It can put things into their proper perspective and give you a reprieve from the daily grind and repetition of life. When you help others, the Universe conspires to help you as well. Some call it the law of karma. Regardless of the terminology, I've seen this time and time again.

If you are feeling down or defeated, volunteer in your community or with your church or food bank. It will turn your whole day around and make you realize that it is good to be blessed but it's better to be a blessing. Now go and share your gifts with the world.

DISCOVERING YOUR PASSION

This world needs you. More than you will ever know. Whenever you need inspiration then read this.

In life, we hear about people's successes far more than their failures. Yet, those who have succeeded have failed far more than anyone knows. Here are just a few examples:

STEVEN SMITH
As an astronaut for NASA, he logged in more than 35 hours in space walks while participating in two different space missions. Yet, the first time he applied to the Space Program they rejected him. He would go on to apply three more times before getting into the Space Program on his fifth attempt.

MILTON HERSHEY
He was a high school dropout who was deemed "a failure" before launching the Hershey Empire and becoming a millionaire.

BABE RUTH struck out more times than he hit home runs.

THE WRIGHT BROTHERS were initially laughed at and ridiculed for their "foolishly absurd ideas and beliefs."

R.H. MACY failed at business seven times before his store in NYC took off and made him an empire.

WALT DISNEY failed at business several times and was forced to file bankruptcy with each failed attempt. The Father of Disneyland was also fired from a job for his lack of "creativity."

LEO TOLSTOY wrote the iconic novel *War and Peace*. While in college, he flunked out and never went back to finish.

THOMAS EDISON is perhaps the most inspiring. He is known as one of the greatest inventors of all time. Yet, he failed over 2,000 times before he finally invented the light bulb. His response was that failure was irrelevant because the creation of the light bulb involved a 2,000-step process.

Therefore, you have 1,999 steps to go.
What are you waiting for, my friend?

CHAPTER TWENTY-NINE

Take Risks

*Great inventions would have never been made,
achievements never reached,
plans faded away had it not been for courage.
Regardless of the outcomes,
all of these had one thing in common.
They started off as risks.*

Often the biggest risk people take in life exists in their unwillingness to take any risks. Risks are a doorway into a different world. A new life. Some of the most successful and happy people would have died miserable and bitter had it not been for their courage to take risks. They believed in themselves and their passions, regardless of the opinions of the outside world.

If you take a risk and fail, at least you can walk away with a clear conscious. Yet, if you *never* take any risks, you have the probability of lying on your deathbed with a lifetime of regrets and broken dreams. This is the greatest risk of all.

I saw this with a necessary caveat, when taking risks, you have to be reasonable. Do not risk your whole house just to become homeless. That is not a risk. That is just stupidity. People confuse risks and stupidity all the time. Stupidity is when you make poor choices that threaten your long-term survival over a short-term gain.

For example, you can start that business. It doesn't mean mortgaging your whole house to do it. Start small. Often times the beginning is the most important because that is where you learn, reassess, become an expert, and evolve your talents. In case it needs repeating - your passions should not make you homeless, jobless, or spouse-less. You can pursue your passions and keep all of these things.

As always, please be reasonable by starting small.

Start today.

Just start.

Even if it is one step.

DISCOVERING YOUR PASSION

Soul's Journal Entry #29

What are the risks you are afraid to take?

_____
_____
_____

What is holding you back? Make a list as detailed as possible.

_____
_____
_____

What are the steps you can take today to eradicate them?

_____
_____
_____

Are you willing to spend a lifetime wondering "what could have been?"

_____
_____
_____

How has this impacted your soul?

_____
_____
_____

DISCOVERING YOUR PASSION

CHAPTER THIRTY

Trust the Universe

*"I read and walked for miles
at night along the beach,
writing bad blank verses and
searching endlessly for someone wonderful
who would step out of the darkness and change my life.
It never crossed my mind that that person could be me."*
~ Anna Quindlen

The most wonderful revelation about discovering and pursing your passion is that the Universe will help. If given enough time and patience, opportunities will arise, people will come into your life. Doorways will begin to open. The Universe will handle the details while you pursue your dreams. Every time you make a "mistake," the Universe will recalculate the best path forward for you (similar to GPS).

Believing that the Universe will assist you is a vital step in discovering your passion. The Universe works for a higher purpose. It is not interested in everyday petty problems or dramas. It is interested in the changes that are eternal and significant. It is interested in the advancement of your soul.

Trusting the Universe also entails listening to the signs that come into your life. These signs may come softly at first, yet, with time they can hold the force of a tornado. They can emerge as positive and negative life forces on your journey.

Whenever you are about to make an important decision ask yourself these simple questions, "Is this bringing me closer or further away from my soul's desire? Is this a betrayal to who I really am or an expression of my truest form?" The answers to these questions can create an outpouring of information and guidance when life presents tough choices. All you need to do is listen and learn.

The realization of trusting the Universe became apparent in my own life. When I began writing this book the most amazing things began to happen. People who could help me in this endeavor found their way into my life. Ideas began pouring out of me. Encouragement came from the most unexpected places – inside my own soul and from strangers.

I never really believed in my ability as a writer. Yet, through the process of writing this book, I began to experience an internal faith that had never existed before. An internal belief that at times became a lifeline. For the first time in my life, I didn't need others to believe in me. I actually believed in myself.

There were also many times when I felt tired and weak inside. Then a voice inside of me would summons me to find the strength to continue writing. Even if it was four in the morning, even if I was surviving only four hours of sleep. The content of this book began pouring out of me. As if the Universe had a hand in it all along.

I also started taking a Life Make Over Class. This class was really an opportunity for a group of women to come together every week and support one another through the trials and tribulations of life. (I've often said there should be a support group just for living life.) I never imagined that a group of strangers would become so instrumental in helping me find and pursue my passion. I never knew that they could become so pivotal in the creation of this book.

In their own unique way, each person helped me by sharing their stories, their wisdom, their pain, and their support for one another. Their time in my life was a complete blessing. They helped this book go from an idea to a reality. They helped me discover my passion. A passion I didn't know exists.

Looking back, I felt more alive writing this book than I ever felt in my life. If I can grant that feeling to just one person then this whole journey has been worth it. None of my struggles have been in vain.

Through this process, I have come to accept that the Universe assists in the most mysterious and unexpected ways. It helps us become closer to our passions. It ultimately helps us find our dreams. Dreams that have been waiting a long time to finally come out.

Soul's Journal Entry #30

How has the Universe helped you in the past?

_____
_____
_____

DISCOVERING YOUR PASSION

Has it brought people, opportunities, wisdom into your life?
_____
_____
_____

How has this changed you?
_____
_____
_____

Have there been time when you have ignored these signs?
_____
_____
_____

How has that impacted your life?
_____
_____
_____

Why did you feel compelled to ignore them?
_____
_____
_____

Did the signs or life lessons resurface in another form years or months later?
_____
_____
_____

DISCOVERING YOUR PASSION

What did you need to learn?

_____
_____
_____
_____
_____

What will you do differently to move forward?

_____
_____
_____
_____
_____

DISCOVERING YOUR PASSION

My Farewell

To any reader who has made it this far – THANK YOU! I leave you with these parting words and hope this book has brought you even half a step closer to your personal dreams or passions. They only belong to you and no one else needs to make sense of it.

To the person reading this:

> In your darkest hour
> I pray that you find light.
> In your saddest moment
> I know you'll find strength.
> In your loneliest day,
> I wish for you friendship.
> During your difficult journey,
> I hope you find some peace.
> And through this life,
> I pray that you find enlightenment
> Because when you finally know your real worth,
> No one can take that from you.

If you have made it this far, thank you for sharing this journey with me. It has been an absolute privilege and honor to walk through this process with you. I can't wait to see what *your* next chapter entails. **You are unstoppable. I believe in you. It's finally your time. What are you waiting for?**

About the Author

Shadan Kapri (pronounced Shadawn Capri) is a U.S. based Attorney, Activist, and Author. Her first book, "The Red Movement: Social and Environmental Justice in the 21st Century" became a Human Rights and Civil Rights Bestseller on Amazon. That book was awarded the *International Impact Book Awards* in March 2024.

She has devoted her life to increasing awareness about women's rights, human rights, and human trafficking. She started that journey in her late 20s and early 30s when she became a U.S. Fulbright Scholar on human trafficking after attending law school. She would go on to work as a law clerk, prosecutor, and private practice attorney. She founded her own legal practice, Kapri Law and Consulting, in her late thirties. Her firm has been recognized on the local and national level for its commitment to women's and children's issues.

Ms. Kapri was born in the Middle East but raised in America. Her parents migrated to the U.S. when she was three years old after the Iranian Revolution. She has written extensively about women's rights in the Middle East and around the world. Her true passion in life is human trafficking awareness. To learn more about her work, please visit www.red-movement.com.

Made in the USA
Columbia, SC
13 May 2024

b6962abd-93e5-445a-b975-7c4cc50145beR01